H. EVAN RUNNER

A Philosopher and Man of God
Scriptural Religion & Political Task

A CELEBRATION OF FAITH SERIES

JOHN HULTINK
H. EVAN RUNNER

"In the American Christian philosopher H. Evan Runner, you will find inspiration, analysis, and a vigorous call to action across the entire range of human experience, all driven by an unwavering commitment to the Word of God."

—Kerry J. Hollingsworth
Former Director of the Reformational Publishing Project and Paideia Press, Grand Rapids, Michigan

"Hultink brings into view who this Christian philosopher was, not just as an academic, but as a person, as a believer firmly committed to thinking Christianly, subject to the Lordship of Christ. Runner was one of the most significant proponents of H. Dooyeweerd's Christian philosophy in North America."

—Rev. Steven R. Martins
Founding Director of the Cántaro Institute; Founding Pastor of Sevilla Chapel, St. Catharines, Ontario

www.cantaroinstitute.org

Published by Cántaro Publications, a publishing imprint of the
Cántaro Institute, 3248 Twenty First St., Jordan Station, ON. L0R
1S0, Canada

Series Editor: Steven R. Martins

Library & Archives Canada
ISBN: 978-1-990771-84-2

Printed in the United States of America

Table of Contents

Series Preface

What is faith? And why should we celebrate it?

OF THE TWO QUESTIONS, the first is the more common; the second, however, is seldom considered, though it should logically follow. In our pluralistic world, the word *faith* has often been used as a token term for all forms of religious belief and expression. You'll find it on bumper stickers, billboards, in books and magazines, and throughout film, music, and media of every kind. *Faith* has come to serve almost as a synonym for *spirituality*—a word that, nowadays, can mean nearly anything. But is this *true* faith? That is, does this represent the genuine definition and understanding of faith in the biblical sense of the term? The short answer is no. Not only does its definition fall short, but its very direction is also misaligned.

What, then, is faith? To understand what faith is—and what it is not—we must first grasp the philosophical concepts of *worldview* and *religion*. When grounded in biblical presuppositions, these concepts provide a logically consistent framework of thought, a set of parameters by which we can faithfully answer such questions. Without this foundation, we are left with a multitude of conflicting definitions and no clear indication of what is true.

First, a *worldview* is something we all possess. It is the lens through which we perceive the world and interpret its facts and evidences. There is not a single living, thinking person who lacks a set of beliefs or presuppositions about reality. As one late apologist defined it, a *worldview* is:

> a network of presuppositions (which are not verified by the procedures of natural science) regarding reality (metaphysics), knowing (epistemology), and conduct (ethics) in terms of which every element of human experience is related and interpreted.[1]

It goes without saying that not every worldview is correct. If one person believes the earth is flat and another believes it is round—and we mean this in the same sense—only one of them can be right. But which one? Every worldview must be tested by two standards: *logical consistency* and *correspondence*. Is the worldview internally coherent? Does it correspond to reality? The Bible, as God's special revelation, provides us with the *true* worldview—a coherent set of presuppositions about reality, knowledge, and ethics that are both logically consistent and correspondent to reality. All other worldviews stand in antithesis to the true one and fail these two tests. Why? Because we live and move and have our being in God's world—and therefore, by necessity, it is a matter of the impossibility of the contrary.[2]

---

1. Gary DeMar, ed., *Pushing the Antithesis: The Apologetic Methodology of Greg L. Bahnsen* (Powder Springs, GA.: American Vision Press, 2010), 42-43.

2. See D. F. M. Strauss, *Being Human in God's World* (Jordan Station, ON.: Paideia Press, 2020).

Second, worldviews are not free or independent from religion. On the contrary, worldview and religion are inseparable. The apostle James wrote to the church, "Religion that is pure and undefiled before God the Father is this: to visit orphans and widows in their affliction, and to keep oneself unstained from the world" (Jas. 1:27). In other words, true religion is to glorify God in all that we do—in every aspect of creational interaction and function. This includes administering the grace of the gospel—the fruit of consecrating the Lord as holy in the very core of our being (1 Pet. 3:15).

Yet just as there is true religion, as defined by God's special revelation, so there is false religion—one that stands in antithesis to the truth, expressed in the worship of creation rather than the Creator (Rom. 1:25). Simply put, our *worldview* is the structure of our presuppositions—what we believe to be true about reality, knowledge, and ethics—while our *religion* is the direction of that structure, our worship. It is the underlying motive rooted in the condition of the human heart.

The reason faith has been defined and understood in so many ways is because it has been interpreted and expressed through a variety of religious worldviews, all of which, apart from Scripture, place a humanistic emphasis on faith's orientation. And while some of these interpretations may contain a trace of truth, they are, as comprehensive systems, fundamentally mistaken.

Having now established the parameters by which these questions can be faithfully addressed—that is, from the standpoint of the biblical religious worldview—we may rightly ask: *What is faith?* And *why should we celebrate it?*

The term *faith*, within the context of biblical Christianity, is conventionally used in at least two distinct senses. According to T*he Oxford Dictionary of the Christian Church*, it is first applied objectively to "the body of truth to be found in the Creeds, in the definitions of accredited Councils, in the teachings of doctors and saints, and, above all, in the revelation contained in the Bible."[3] In other words, it refers to the religious worldview of Christianity itself.

Within this *objective* faith, there is, secondly, the *subjective* faith—what Paul identifies in 1 Corinthians 13:13 as one of the three theological virtues, alongside hope and love. *The Oxford Dictionary* explains that this faith "is the human response to Divine truth, inculcated in the Gospels as the childlike and trusting acceptance of the Kingdom [of God] and its demands, and known as 'the faith whereby belief is reached' (*fides qua creditor*)."[4]

Whereas other religious worldviews emphasize subjective faith as a natural human act, and in their case, it is in fact a *false* faith because it is placed in something other than the Creator, Scripture teaches that faith is a *supernatural* act. In other words, a Christian possesses *true* faith only as the result of God's regenerative work in the heart (Ezek. 36:26–27; Jn. 1:12–13; 3:3–8; Tit. 3:5). Simply stated, *subjective faith* is the gift of God that enables one to embrace the *objective faith* of God's revealed truth.

---

3. F. L. Cross, ed., *The Oxford Dictionary of the Christian Church*, second edition (Toronto, ON.: Oxford University Press, 1974), 499.
4. Ibid.

Why must faith be an external gift? Because man, in his sin, cannot of his own volition turn to God in repentance and faith. His sinful disposition prevents this (Jn. 8:34; Rom. 6:20; 2 Tim. 2:25–26; Tit. 3:3). This is not to suggest that man is incapable of making choices between life and death (Deut. 30:15–20), but rather that his will is enslaved to sin and therefore unable to choose *life*—that is, the life found in Jesus Christ—unless he is first liberated from this bondage (2 Chron. 6:36; Job 14:4; Prov. 20:9; Eccl. 7:20; Jer. 13:23; Jn. 6:65). Left to himself, man will always choose death, for he is by nature hostile to the truth of God (Gen. 6:5; Jn. 8:44; Rom. 1:18; 8:7–8; Eph. 4:17–19).

Deliverance from this fallen condition is ultimately the work of the Spirit of God, who removes the heart of stone and replaces it with a heart of flesh (Ezek. 36:26). Having been freed from captivity, man—now renewed in heart—is able to make the only logical and spiritually possible choice before him: faith in the Lord and Saviour Jesus Christ, and all that such faith entails (Acts 11:18; 13:48; Eph. 2:8–9; Phil. 1:29; 2 Tim. 2:25–26).

This is precisely why so many different religious worldviews exist in our day. Sin has not only caused our alienation from God and our spiritual death; it has also affected—or, we might say, *infected*—the totality of our being, including our intellectual and mental faculties: what theologians call the *noetic effects of sin*. Instead of interpreting God's general revelation in creation as it truly is, our fallen and hostile nature suppresses the truth and fashions false worldviews filled with inevitable god-substitutes (Rom. 1:18, 25).

It is for this very reason that God has given the special revelation of His Word as the only authoritative interpretation of His created reality—for without it, we would be as blind men groping in the dark. But when God, by His irresistible grace, draws men and women to Himself, these false god-substitutes are abandoned *by* faith in exchange for the *true* faith. As John Newton (1725–1807) wrote in his timeless hymn *Amazing Grace*, "I once was lost, but now am found; was blind, but now I see."

If, therefore, saving faith originates from God—for how else can man be saved?—then a celebration of faith is not merely a celebration of what we believe or of what God has revealed (though that, in itself, is worthy of praise), but above all, a celebration of what God has done to redeem sinful wretches such as ourselves. And what greater reason do we need to celebrate faith than this: that Christ has offered Himself as the ultimate sacrifice to save us from our fallen condition and from the judgment that awaits the living and the dead (2 Tim. 4:1; 1 Pet. 4:5–6)?

Not only has He rescued us from darkness by forgiving our sin—having paid its penalty through His death (1 Cor. 6:20; Eph. 1:7; 1 Pet. 1:18–19; 1 Jn. 2:2; Rev. 5:9)—He has also reconciled us to the Father and begun in us the work of renewal and restoration. By the sanctifying power of the Spirit, He restores us to our original state of righteousness and to our creational purpose.

If our created purpose, as *The Westminster Confession of Faith* declares, is to glorify God and to delight in Him forever (Rom. 11:36; 1 Cor. 10:31; Ps. 73:24–26; Jn. 17:22, 24), how could this be possible without faith? For, as the author of Hebrews writes, "without faith it is impossible to please God" (Heb. 11:6).

This, too, is why we celebrate faith: not only because God has granted us the gift of saving faith, but because faith itself enables us to fulfill our highest end—to glorify God and to delight in Him forever. To celebrate faith, then, is ultimately to celebrate the glory of God Himself, for true faith, rooted in God's Word, comes only from Him, the "author and finisher of our faith" (Heb. 12:2).

A Celebration of Faith is a series that reflects on the lives and contributions of those who have been touched by the grace of God—men and women who have professed, defended, and advanced the Christian religious worldview. Though there are countless stories to be told, the editorial team behind this series has sought to highlight certain saints who have inspired generations to live lives of steadfast faith, as well as others whose witness, though largely forgotten, left a profound mark on the culture of their time. The purpose of this series is to inspire and encourage grace-redeemed believers to live out their faith in a manner that manifests the truth, beauty, and freedom of the gospel—demonstrating its all-encompassing power for the advancement of God's kingdom.

Profiled in this volume is the late American philosopher H. Evan Runner (1916–2002). Runner was the foremost North American representative of *The Philosophy of the Law-Idea*—that comprehensive Christian philosophy inaugurated by Herman Dooyeweerd and D. H. Th. Vollenhoven. Penetrating, prophetic, and profoundly insightful are but a few of the terms used to describe this remarkable Reformational scholar, whose call to action extended across the entire spectrum of human experience, grounded in an unwavering commitment to the Word of God.

Several of Runner's lectures and writings have been published, including his *Unionville Lectures* on the *Relation of the Bible to Learning*. This present volume features his *Lectures on Scriptural Religion and Political Task*, preceded by a personable introduction by John Hultink, founder of Book Depot and Paideia Press, who studied under Runner during his years at Calvin College. H. Evan Runner—a Reformational philosopher and intellectual trailblazer in his own right—stands as an exemplary figure of faith, eminently worthy of being profiled in this series.

It is our hope that the Lord will use this book to cultivate within the church a deeper appreciation for our Christian heritage—for we have inherited a great treasure in the faith into which we have been redeemed. May you be inspired through this profile to live out your faith with boldness, undaunted by the challenges and afflictions of life in a fallen world, confident that the Lord will sustain you as you seek to be the salt and light of the earth (Matt. 5:13–16). And may you be both equipped and informed concerning the church's mission: to preserve and advance biblical truth, not only in its confession but also in its faithful application—for the growth of God's kingdom and for His glory alone.

May God be glorified,

The Editorial Team
Cántaro Publications

A Philosopher and Man of God

John Hultink

0.1 A Personal Student Experience

H. EVAN RUNNER WAS A CHARACTER. His personal traits and de-
meanor made quite an impression on a classroom full of fresh-
man college students about to participate in their first course
in philosophy. In my mind's eye, I can still see him standing
there behind the lectern, twirling his glasses and gesticulating.
By the time I arrived at Calvin College in the fall of '64, Runner had been teaching there for thirteen years and had perfect-
ed his technique. He was a natural teacher. And what a teacher
he was. A gifted communicator.

Runner had no difficulty making our first day in his philosophy class a memorable one. After some introductory remarks about what he hoped to achieve during the course of
the semester, he informed the class that what he expected each
student to achieve by the end of the term was to submit a paper
answering the enquiry, "What is a thing?" I could not believe
it. How do you answer a question like that? What thing? There
are a million things. At first I thought that perhaps it was a
trick question. Or perhaps one of those really deep questions
a psychology professor once posed to his graduate students on
their final exam when he wrote on the blackboard, "Why?",

and left the room, leaving the students to figure it out. After the better part of an hour's reflection, the brightest student in the class wrote, "Why Not?", handed in his exam paper and later received an A for his effort.

It became apparent, during the course of the semester, that there would be no two-word answers to Runner's enquiry, "What is a thing?", when our professor began lecturing about the "structure of creation," "cosmic modalities," "subject and object relationships," and "anticipatory and retrocipatory moments." Well, at least I had an answer to the question as to what the difference is between high school and college. And over 50 years later, as I write these words and am rapidly moving toward the "higher reality" that Evan Runner has achieved, I now also realize that no one other than God will ever have the definitive answer to what a "thing" really is.

Runner's classes were never boring. He constantly had our heads spinning, our hearts pumping and our spirits soaring. Runner was a man with a mission. That was another thing that was apparent that first day in his philosophy class. This was not just another course in yet one more class. This was a man with a mission, and this man was looking for converts. It would not be an overstatement to say that what H. Evan Runner hoped to achieve in his lifetime was the de-secularization or better, the Christianization, of higher education. Toward that goal Runner dedicated his life.

And toward that goal Runner inspired his students to become participants in the various sciences to reclaim them in the name of the Lordship of Jesus Christ. It is why many of Runner's students became professors at Christian colleges, teachers at Christian grade and high schools, ministers and leaders in various Christian cultural organizations. In some respects, Runner's influence extended to students around the globe, directly or indirectly. Even Chuck Colson, president of Prison Fellowship, came under Evan's influence. And learned to love Kuyper.

I became one of Runner's converts. I may not have been one of his brightest students, though I certainly became one of his most ardent disciples. That was one of Evan's many gifts – helping students come to grips with their calling in life. There was nothing that Evan Runner would not do for "his students" to further that end. To some he gave a roof and shelter; to exceptional students, private tutorials; with others he would sit for hours in the campus coffee shop assisting them in their studies and careers; to all he was an inspiration and willing friend.

Never will I forget the day when my turn came to prepare a paper for the Groen Club – the locals' term for the student club named for the nineteenth-century Dutch politician and scholar Guillaume Groen van Prinsterer. The combination of joy and anxiety could not have been greater if I had been asked to escort the queen to the student prom. Runner genuinely loved his students; Runner was also a hard taskmaster. Runner did not suffer fools or foolish insights gladly. And there was no higher calling during four years of college life for a "Runner student" than to succeed admirably in the writing and presentation of his Groen Club paper. Dr. Tunis Prins, another of my Calvin philosophy professors, who was of the opinion that Plato was a Christian 400 years before Christ's incarnation, would have to spend most of the semester looking at my empty seat.

So I went to see Dr. Runner at his home to review the assignment ("The Nature of Revelation"), and to ask him for copies of old Groen Club papers written by some of his better students to help me come to grips with my assignment. As usual, Runner dropped whatever he was doing and went to collect an armful of student papers. This meeting with Dr. Runner was helpful, but it did nothing to arrest my anxiety. He extracted a student paper from the pile and said, "Here is an example, John, of what you do not want to do." The title of this particular student paper was something like, "Calling, Task and Culture." Dr. Runner then went on to explain that this otherwise capable student had made the fatal error of confusing *vice-gerent* with *vice-regent* – spoiling the entire paper. For Dr. Runner, teaching was not solely a classroom affair. Wherever two or three are gathered together, there he would teach. So he proceeded to teach.

"A vice-regent, John, is someone who acts in the place of a ruler, like the vice-president of the United States who acts in the place of the president when he is unconscious or dead. We do not act in God's place. God is sovereign; always present, always sovereign. Christians are always and everywhere God's vice-gerents. All our authority, all our power, is delegated to us by God, who is the ruler and supreme head. So we do not act in God's place, for God has not relinquished His sovereignty, nor, contrary to popular academic opinion, is God dead; our human acts are always and everywhere acts in response to the mandate God has delegated us to perform. CORAM DEO! So you see, John, that we are God's vice-gerents; not His vice-regents." I saw. And I went home, in fear and trembling, to write a Groen Club paper on "The Nature of Revelation." As I walked back to my residence, I whispered, "And God help me, if I get it wrong." Besides Dr. Prins' class, I would have to find a few more non-essential classes to skip.

What was it that inspired such dedication in Runner's students? What drove his students to the outer limits of their abilities? Runner was very fatherly in recognizing a student's abilities. He never asked a student to perform beyond the talents God had given that student. And those talents varied widely. But the admiration and dedication on the part of the students did not. Why was that?

0.2 Popular Philosophy and Missionary Zeal

The breadth and depth of the Christian insight formulated by Herman Dooyeweerd and Dirk Vollenhoven and their academic associates, which became known by the name the Philosophy of the Law-Idea, does not readily lend itself to popularization. And unlike Camus' and Sartre's existentialism, does not readily absorb itself into the public psyche. What does lend itself to popularization and broad public comprehension is the *religious dynamic* of the Philosophy of the Law-Idea. No one understood this better than H. Evan Runner, who as a young man had a driving passion to go to Korea or China as God's missionary. With the northern march of the communists and the demise of the Kuomintang in the late '40s this was not advisable.[1] (Think of Steve McQueen in "The Sand Pebbles.")

---

1. Harry Van Dyke and Albert M. Wolters, "Interview with Dr. H. Evan Runner" in *Hearing and Doing: Philosophical Essays Dedicated to H. Evan Runner*, ed. John Kraay and Anthony Tol (Toronto, ON.: Wedge

That missionary zeal which failed to find its outlet in the fields of Korea and China, Evan Runner brought with him into the classroom. When he had completed his doctoral studies and years of preparation teaching high school students Greek and Latin, the fertile fields of Calvin College, with its thousands of students and scores of professors, became his mission field. Like most missionaries, Evan Runner was not always warmly received. Especially not after he gave a public address entitled, "Rudder, Hard Over,"[2] the intent of which was clear, even to the unsuspecting. This public speech was a not-so-subtle criticism of the academic direction that Runner saw Calvin College taking.

The students loved it. Here was a man who shared their youthful idealism, unfettered on their part by bitter experience; here was a man who breathed a warmth and a power into his presentation of the Word of God that few had witnessed from the pulpit.

Evan Runner took his students by the hand and led them to a field where lay hidden a treasure of such magnitude, it defied human comprehension. Evan Runner, a man who did barely a stitch of physical labor during his entire 86 years on earth, took hold of a shovel and excavated that field until that exquisite treasure lay exposed for all his students to behold. "Here," he said, like a proud father at the birth of his child, "this is the kingdom of God. Sell everything you own and everything you desire to own in this life that beckons you. Aban-

---

Publishing Foundation, 1979), 337.

2.   H. Evan Runner, "Het Roer Om" (Rudder Hard Over), *Torch and Trumpet 3* (April-May 1953): 1-4.

don your dreams of personal glory and greatness, riches and wealth; relinquish your self-centered ambitions and aspirations and join me for the rest of your lives to labor in the vineyard of the Lord."

Missionary zeal in and of itself would not have been enough for Runner to inspire his students and extract a commitment from them which few professors, (Calvin Seerveld was another) anywhere in North America could match. What Runner accomplished in his lifetime through his students is unusual in the extreme.

0.3 The Battle for Ultimate Allegiance

The reason for Runner's success with his students was this: Runner was a committed Christian, teaching Christian students, at a Christian liberal arts college. When Runner, the professor, stood in front of the class looking at all those students, he saw himself, so to speak, sitting among his students. Runner was one of us. He knew our needs before we did; he understood our deepest conflicts before we gave voice to them; he already knew how we struggled in the depths of our being to attempt to relate our Christian faith to learning. He knew that the college's claim of offering students unity in diversity (say uni-versity) was false. Stones for bread. He knew because he had walked in our shoes, struggled with our questions, lived with our frustrations. He understood us; knew exactly where to take us.

About his own education, which included three years at Harvard and exposure to some of the finest humanist minds of his day, Runner stated in an interview in 1979: "I was becoming a bit skeptical about the meaning of my research projects. I was just accumulating facts, facts, facts, but my ability to unify them and see sense in them was not keeping pace.... My life was just a lot of bits and pieces; it wasn't pulled together."[3] Sentiments every college and university student can relate to. And this Evan Runner understood and appreciated.

About his experiences at the University of Pennsylvania, Runner stated the following:

> I had a year course in modern philosophy from Henry Bradford Smith, one of America's best logicians. He was the one who at the end of the first lecture dared us to leave the faith of our homes behind us and follow the course with an open mind. He said, 'This class is made up of all kinds of people – orthodox Protestants, Orthodox Jews, liberal Jews, Roman Catholics, Greek Orthodox Christians, and unbelievers like myself. How can we possibly discuss together unless we have some common basis? And since it can't be any of those things, what else is there except that we can build a fund of rational ideas together? And that's what modern philosophy is all about.' Well, I was impressed with that. That's the day I walked home through the park and stood in front of a tree and took out my pocketknife and scratched my initials in the tree and thought: 'Do I dare or don't I dare?' I finally decided I didn't dare let go of my faith. I learned from that later how important it is to grasp a student in the first week – when those fundamental decisions are being made that determine the whole direction of his life.[4]

That day in 1935, at the University of Pennsylvania, in Henry Bradford Smith's class, was the turning point in young Evan's life; it was the day God decreed to take control of the young student's life and save him from himself. It was the day

---

3. Van Dyke and Wolters, "Interview with Dr. H. Evan Runner," 346.

4. Ibid., 338-339.

God decreed that Howard Evan Runner would become His missionary to students at Calvin College and elsewhere.

Which serious student, at one point or another in his life, has not stood alongside Evan in that park, carving his initials into that tree, to weigh his allegiances to God's great adversary? "Give up your faith in God, empty your mind of everything your mother taught you about God as you sat on her knee, abandon the faith of your home, and come, follow me, on this exciting, humanist experiment." Which of us has not faced that temptation – even in the sanctity of the Christian classroom?

On that day, God said: "No, Evan. You will not eat the poisonous fruit from Henry Bradford Smith's tree. Go. Carve your initials into that tree; carve them deep into your mind as well, so that this act may become a lasting memorial to you of My covenant faithfulness. The cry of your young heart, that I reveal to you the relationship of My Word to learning, has been answered. I will send you to Westminster Theological Seminary; there you will meet My servant, Cornelius Van Til. At Westminster, I will introduce you to My 'blustering' servant, Klaas Schilder. Then I will send you to the Free University founded by My servant, Abraham Kuyper. There you will find My faithful servants, Vollenhoven and Dooyeweerd. They will provide you with the tools required to perform the task I have decreed for you."

Evan Runner's academic experiences, his youthful exposure, during the formative years of his life, to Henry Bradford Smith; his probing search to forge unity into the segmentation of his academic endeavours; the unifying power of the Word of God as he came to understand the coherence of God's creation under Van Til, Schilder, Vollenhoven, Dooyeweerd – these all served to make Evan Runner a man of God, missionary to countless students.

Yes, Howard Evan Runner understood his students better than they understood themselves. Runner, the professor, saw himself in every student he ever taught. He understood the perils those students faced when they set foot on campus. He knew: The tree with his initials loomed ever larger in his memory. God would never let Evan forget.

"Do I dare or don't I dare to let go of my faith?" Evan understood the terrifying struggle that engages every student in the battle of the spirits. "Is it really imperative, dear God, that I must choose between academic respectability in the eyes of my worldly colleagues and faithfulness to You?" He understood and it became his mission in life to take as many of those students as God would grant him, and lead them to that field where lay hidden that great treasure.

Students sensed Runner's uncompromising commitment; they realized that this man believed what he said. Teaching was not merely a means to earn a livelihood for Evan Runner. It was his life. He lived and breathed his convictions. At times, the Spirit who propelled Evan Runner became palpable in his words. One such time was on the occasion of the opening of the Institute for Christian Studies, where Evan Runner gave the keynote address. Runner's grasp of history is comprehensive. And in the opening of the Institute he saw the efforts and blessings of a lifetime come together. As he spoke, his words vibrated with a holy passion:

What a day this is to be alive! How full of consequences for the life of future generations! How crucial for all the English-speaking nations, and even, as we hope, for far beyond! We come today introducing into the life of this nation and of this continent a new institution. More weighty is the fact that for the English-speaking world it is even a new, an unheard-of kind of institution. The emergence of this new thing means that a new concentration of forces is taking shape. It signifies a re-organization of our human and material resources to accomplish a task not yet undertaken. There is a realignment with the avowed purpose of carrying out the Christian mission in higher education in a manner and to a degree never hitherto attempted on our continent. This is a radical Christian proposal for radical times. Karl Marx is justly celebrated for his remark: 'To be radical is to go to the root of the question. Now the root of mankind is man.' Since Marx, all of us are being driven more and more to the root of the question. Our attention is now going to have to be centered upon things which previously, if they have been given any consideration at all, have been considered only very incidentally and peripherally. This charting of a new course is what clearly marks the event we are witnessing here today as an historic event. Events of this kind are to be experienced only very infrequently.... Today, on this high day of our own corporate life, what high privilege it is to be alive and present in this chamber! Such a rush of feelings and sentiments surges through us, now that we are come to this moment! Above all else, we are grateful to God on high, that He still, at a late hour in our history, graciously grants us the historical freedom to take this significant and decisive step that we are taking here this day.[5]

---

5. Runner, "Point Counter Point," An address delivered on October 7, 1967, in Toronto, on the occasion of the opening of the Institute for Christian Studies.

After two thousand years of Christianity, what is this "new thing" that Evan Runner was talking about? What is this "Christian mission in higher education in a manner and to a degree never hitherto attempted on our continent"? The answer to that question is the answer to Runner's success with his students.

0.4 Life Is Religion

The institution that became the exclusive, dominant voice of Christianity in the Western world for more than a millennium, the Roman Catholic Church, and in a real sense, our Mother, got it fundamentally wrong. Under the influence of Greek philosophy, the Roman Catholic Church developed a view of reality (life) which effectively divided the life of the Christian into two compartments: the compartments of **a)** nature and **b)** grace. Among evangelical Christians this compartmentalization is better known as the **a)** secular and **b)** religious. Opponents of Christianity never tire of pointing out that "religion" is for the church and, perhaps, for the home. But religion has no place in the public affairs of mankind. Runner radically broke with this dualistic view of life; this idea that there is a domain of nature, the secular domain, where Christians and non-Christians have everything in common.

Runner coined the phrase: Life Is Religion. (The insight underlying this phrase did not originate with Runner, just the phrase.) The assertion that "Life is Religion" is based on the insight that faith is a human function. It is common for unbelievers to contend that Christians have faith; unbelievers, atheists, agnostics, pagans do not. Such is not the case. Faith is as much a human function as is reasoning. To live out of one's faith is man's inescapable condition. No one acquainted with the writings of Bertrand Russell would accuse Russell of being a Christian. But Russell wore his faith on his sleeve. Russell believed passionately in human freedom, human autonomy. Freedom and autonomy were the shrines at which Russell worshiped. In his book, *Why I Am Not a Christian*, Russell wrote an article entitled "A Free Man's Worship." Is not this Russell's creed when he proclaims:

> Brief and powerless is man's life; on him and all his race the slow, sure doom falls pitiless and dark. Blind to good and evil, reckless of destruction, omnipotent matter rolls on its relentless way; for man, condemned today to lose his dearest, tomorrow himself to pass through the gates of darkness, it remains only to cherish, ere yet the blow fall, the lofty thoughts that ennoble his little day; disdaining the coward terrors of the slave of Fate, to worship at the shrine that his own hands have built...[6]

Russell was not a Christian, though he did have *faith*. Only instead of worshipping the true God, Russell "worships at the shrine his own hands have built." As do all who do not worship the true God who revealed Himself in Scripture (cf. Isa. 44:8b – "You are my witnesses. Is there any God besides me? No, there is no other rock; I know not one.")

Evan Runner never tired of pointing out to his students that all men are religious. It is man's inescapable condition, as Russell has so eloquently demonstrated. When Henry Bradford Smith dared the young Evan Runner and his fellow classmates

---

6. Bertrand Russell, "A Free Man's Worship" in *Why I Am Not a Christian, and Other Essays on Religion and Related Topics* (New York: Simon and Schuster, 1957), 115-116.

to abandon their respective faiths and approach the study of modern philosophy "with an open mind" he was, in fact, selling all his students a bill of goods. It was deception of the worst kind by an individual in a position of power and trust. What Henry Bradford Smith actually asked his students to do was to place their trust in so-called autonomous human reason, the faith to which Smith himself subscribed.

Runner helped his students to see that our lives are made of whole cloth. There are no seams, no dualisms. Either man stands in service of the true God or he worships an idol. But worship someone or something, he will. Therefore, it is imperative for Christians to discard the false dualism of nature and grace as articulated by the Roman Catholic Church. The whole man is religious and life in its entirety is a walk before the face of God, in obedience or disobedience. Nature and grace do not stand in opposition to each other. Faith (grace) is not a super-added gift. It is man's creaturely condition. At issue is whether that faith is directed at God or at an idol. The insight that "life in its entirety is religion" (CORAM DEO), throws a "new" light on our understanding of the entire human enterprise.

Once Runner convinced the Christian student that "Life is Religion" and that all men are at heart religious beings serving either the true God or an idol, the question followed: "What implications does this have for a Christian worldview, a Christian philosophy? The answer is indeed radical, does indeed go to the root of the question. For fallen man it means that God's revelation of Himself must of necessity form the foundation of all human scholarship. Vollenhoven and Dooyeweerd acknowledged this radical belief in their formulation of the "Philosophy of the Law-Idea." That philosophy itself is worthy of an article, but it is anchored in three profoundly confessional statements. The first is that God is Creator; the second, that the human race, through its representative head, Adam, fell into sin; and the third, that all those who confess the name of Christ, the new Adam and representative head, are granted new life in this life and the next.

This "new thing" that Evan Runner refers to in his keynote address at the opening of the Institute for Christian Studies (ICS) is an academic enterprise that is based on a biblically informed understanding of man and the creation. It was indeed a new thing. I know of no other academic enterprise that declares that all of created reality – God's cosmos – can only be properly understood on the rock-solid basis of a confession that

1: God created the cosmos out of nothing

2: He placed man (Adam) at the head of that creation as steward, but Adam became a rebel and served Satan

3: Christ took Adam's place and redirected the entire creation back to God

Law, as understood by the formulators of the Philosophy of the Law-Idea, is an expression of God's will (Rev. 11:4). Law, in the form of God speaking, is the divine mechanism whereby He commanded the entire creation into existence. At the heart of this "new thing" lies our understanding of this biblical idea of law.

I have always considered the most important insight Dr. Runner taught to be his explanation of law. In his book *The*

Relation of the Bible to Learning, he writes: "Law is every Word of God by which He has subjected the creation to His will or rule. Law is thus nothing other than the will of the Sovereign God for creation."[7] Rooted in this understanding of Law, the Philosophy of the Law-Idea worked out a biblical understanding of the unity and diversity of all that God created. This understanding of law opens a window to viewing creation as it has never been understood before. This foundational view of the law "enables" us to "grasp" the biblical revelation found in Colossians 1:16-17: "For by him all things were created: things in heaven and on earth, visible and invisible, whether thrones or powers or rulers or authorities; all things were created by him and for him."

In an attempt to share his insight into God's law with his audience on the occasion of the opening of the ICS, Dr. Runner stated,

> God's Law is God's Word. Because God is God, His every Word is Law. For the very first words of the Bible we hear, "And God said, 'Let there be'" this and that. All such creative words are the Law. The Law is what causes creatures and the whole creation to hang together; it determines the condition of all creaturely existence. It itself is concentrated in the religious Law of life: Walk before Me according to My commandments and live (cf. 1 Kgs. 3:14). Here we have the heart of the creation. The Law determines what it means to live before God, or to die before God. The Jews were the people of God's choice. He made Himself known to them; to them He gave Himself. They were His people and He was their God. He was with them and for them.

---

7. Runner, *The Relation of the Bible to Learning* (Toronto, ON: Wedge Publishing, 1970), 50.

The Law simply gives expression to this covenantal fellowship. It is the Word of the living God by which the people of His choice live before His face, by which they are enabled to bring all the potentialities and capacities which God Himself has laid in human existence, both individual and collective, to the fullest and richest possible realization in a service of God. This is the true Kingdom of God, and here is the true *joie de vivre* (joy of life) which makes one to dance before Jehovah.[8]

In an attempt to illustrate the life-giving power of God's Law, Runner quotes the example used by R.B. Kuiper who tells the story of the slightly peculiar old lady who went to visit a friend.

When her hostess disappeared into the kitchen for a few minutes, the peculiar old lady got out of her chair, and walking about the salon, found a bowl of tropical fish behind the grand piano. In a sudden inspiration she reached her hand into the bowl, lifted out one of the fish and dropped him tenderly onto the rich carpeting that covered the floor. As she did so she muttered to herself, 'Wicked old woman, keeping you shut up in that little old bowl! I'm going to give you the freedom of this whole salon.'

Runner, who quotes this illustration in his book, *The Relation of the Bible to Learning*, goes on to note:

Of course, the fish promptly proceeded to expire. Why? Because it had been removed from that law area for which God had created it. And so it is also with man: he can be free to live as man only when he is in the Law-environment for which he was created. That 'environment' is the full range of the divine Law for the creation, is every Law-word that proceeds out of the mouth of God. In this sense, the Law (God's will) is the condition of

---

man's freedom.

As an expression of God's will, God's rule, Law is the only key that will open our minds to understanding creation in all its unity and diversity as created by God.

0.5 Afterthought

A few weeks ago, I visited my old friend, Henry VanderGoot, in Grand Rapids, Runner's hometown. As we were reminiscing over supper, we recalled some of our Calvin College experiences. "You know," Henry said, "it is almost 55 years ago, John, that we, as freshmen, sat in Runner's course: Philosophy 101. We are now well into our seventies. Most of life lies behind us. Was there any one single event in our entire lives that was more meaningful and provided us with more insight, in terms of grappling with the unity and diversity of creation than that one single course, in Runner's class where we struggled to come to terms with the question: What is a thing?"

Do you understand this, dear readers, as you yourself attempt to come to terms with reality in the 21st century? Do you comprehend what a priceless gift Evan Runner bequeathed to his students? A gift that served them well all the days of their lives. That gift, that legacy, is now made accessible to us, for example, through the Canadian organization of the Ezra Institute based in Grimsby, Ontario, and the numerous reformational publications of Paideia Press.

You cannot sit in on Dr. Runner's lectures. Evan Runner has gone to be with his Lord and Saviour. If Christ is your Lord and Saviour also, you will see Evan Runner at the great and wondrous resurrection that is rapidly approaching. But some of the fruits of our lives outlive us. Such was the case in Dr. Runner's life.

The day young Evan stood in the park, considered his professor's proposal to abandon his Christian faith, and carved his initials into that tree is now 84 years ago – years that bear witness to God's profound love and covenant faithfulness. In God's merciful providence, and to your great benefit, Evan Runner himself became like a tree – a tree planted by streams of living water, which yielded its fruit in season. Great and blessed was the company of those who ate freely from that tree. Thankful are they to have carved their initials therein.

Scriptural Religion & Political Task

H. Evan Runner

1.0 Preface

I AM PLEASED TO KNOW that these lectures, presented under
the auspices of the A.R.S.S. which is now known as the Association for the Advancement of Christian Scholarship, are to
be made available once again. They were written, it should be
remembered, in the summer of 1961, thus close to 15 years
ago, and I should like to see some things changed, some omitted, and some even slightly enlarged. Nevertheless, since that
possibility does not exist at present, I want to state that over the
years my conviction has only strengthened that the course here
initiated was right, and I fervently hope that more and more of
my fellow-believers, now more thoroughly alerted to the true
state of affairs by the events of the past decade and a half, will
come to see that our political institutions are not just there, as a
potato is there (in which case Christians could do nothing but
accept the established political framework, their Christianity
affecting nothing more than their action as individuals within
it), but that political parties, systems of political parties (e.g.,
the two-party system), and the rest of our political structures
(e.g., majority government or proportional representation) are
themselves different than a potato; these structures and move-

ments too are the result of human beliefs and of human willing and acting. Political scientists who are Christians often speak of the position developed in these lectures as visionary and idealistic, and claim it to be realistic to accept political structures as given, as the "hard facts of political life", as the "pragmatics" of the situation. Such men recommend running for office on the precinct level within one of the "established" parties, for example. I believe that that attitude is not something that characterizes the knowledgeable political scientist, but is the confusion brought about in his mind by his uncritical acceptance of the political science taught in our universities. For there is a philosophy operative at the foundation of every special science, thus also of the political science taught in our universities, and that philosophy for a long time now has been positivism, a naturalism that does indeed confuse such things as political structures and a potato. To make matters worse, positivism insists that the special sciences have no need of a philosophy, that they begin where our experience begins, with the facts (thus ignoring the abstraction involved in getting from things experienced directly to the data of the several special sciences). Thus, political scientists often mistakenly ascribe to their special science what is due only to the operation of a positivistic philosophic commitment within their scientific work. But they do not distinguish the two. Christians who are trained political scientists may often therefore offer the strongest resistance to what I have written. I can only hope and pray that they will do here what every Christian must always do, in every life situation, namely, listen carefully and make a spiritual judgment about the analysis here presented. That is what we all must do. And, to do it, we need to understand two things: (1) the meaning of our life as a walk with God in His Covenant (which has been revealed to us in the Scripture); (2) the religious direction of what has happened in history to give us the political structures and movements we are confronted with (to determine which, the Spirit of God works in His people the mind of Christ). Individualism – that all we have to do is see to it that Christian individuals are elected to the structures we have inherited and within the parties representing the movements that have arisen in the course of our political history – this individualism is not enough. It is a prevalent American cultural attitude, but it is not sufficiently Christian. The election of Christian individuals within the present system will get us nowhere, because it does not yet deal with the real sickness, which is: living our political life apart from our one, undivided life in God's Covenant according to the Word by which He created the world. Groen van Prinsterer, a great Dutch Christian statesman of the middle 19th century, predicted, three years before the publication of the *Communist Manifesto*, that, as the conditions of life worsened, the western world would move from conservatism to liberalism to a radicalism of a humanistic sort (e.g., communism). A remarkable prophecy! Political half-way stations are not going to be of any help to us in our present crisis. We need, as Marx said, to be radical and get to the root of man's life. The only question is where we will derive our knowledge of man, from our own rationality and experience, as Marx did, or from the Word of the living God. We need men and women to live politically out of a whole-hearted commitment to Jesus Christ and the whole revealed Word of God. Then, perhaps, the present young political revolutionaries – and there will be more of them – will learn to fight for political, social and economic justice on the side of the Lord of Creation, whose Kingdom will surely come, and is coming daily through our own acts of obedience to His revealed Word.

July, 1974

Lecture I:
THESIS

1.1 Its Political Articulation

MR. CHAIRMAN, FOR THE THIRD successive year I have the honour of being one of your lecturers here at the Unionville Conference. I want you and the whole Board of Trustees of our Association for Reformed Scientific Studies to know how deeply grateful I am for the confidence you have thus repeatedly shown in the work I have been doing here, and for the opportunity I have been given to share in a significant way in the development of this movement.

I alone, of your speakers, have had the wonderful privilege of seeing this Conference grow to what, in the brief span of these three years, it has already become. When I speak of the growth of our Unionville Conference I do not think first of numbers, although numerical growth is not without its importance. What to me has been so very remarkable about these conferences is the evident spiritual hunger and thirst of our Christian students for a truly biblically directed scholarship, your spiritual eagerness, élan and vigor, and the substantial growth in our collective understanding of our life as religion. I should like to have you know, Mr. Chairman, that the experiences I have had at these conferences I count among the most precious of my life.

1.2 General Introduction

We must thank God and take courage. There can no longer be any doubt about it: the signs multiply almost daily which indicate that, whereas in large areas of Christendom the Christian Cause languishes and grows weak from lack of a determination (born always, of course, of faith) to live integrally by the light of the Word of God, and from an almost eager accommodation to the ways (of thought and of action) of the world round about, God has been pleased in our midst to perform a mighty work. In these conferences we are experiencing a recovery of the Word of God in its integral meaning as directing Principle of our whole life, of our "walk" in life, that is of our life-dynamics. Specifically, as students we have been brought to view the whole of the scientific enterprise as a "moment" of our religion, as one particular manner of our *whole*-hearted response to God Who addresses us in His Word.

Everywhere in the world there are hosts of Christians who have learned how to "use" the Scripture to prove this or that point in Roman Catholic or Arminian, Lutheran or Calvinist theology. There are also a great many Christian students who are seemingly content to memorize, more or less, the materials of their several sciences, in whatever form these materials may have come to assume in the historical development of the modern secular mind – as though scientific thought, and the results obtained thereby, were autonomous, i.e. unrelated to the root-"seeing," the root-"experiencing" of *religious* persons – , at best hemming in such (scripturally) "unreformed" areas of scientific thought with certain propositions borrowed from the (more or less scripturally-directed) science of theology – so-called *theologische Lehnsatze* – in an ill-fated effort to limit the range of influence of the powerful religious drive of apostasy operative in them.

1.3 Reason to Thank God

But how few there are who have come, as we have here, to experience the integral driving power of the divine Word in the innermost root (heart) of our existence, so that the entirety of our life-expression (our acts, both thought-acts or theory and so-called practical acts) will be directed by that selfsame Word! And what is this blessed thing that we have been experiencing here at this place if not a re-discovery of the Biblical "hearing and doing," if not a recovery of the deepest intention of the reformation movements of Luther and Calvin? For these reformers too life is religion. God is there first, and He called man into being to "walk" before Him as servant in loving obedience, to worship and serve Him in the administration of the earth in a variety of offices. This is the meaning of the reformation's *coram Deo vivere*. That God has been pleased to open our hearts to understand once again this integral sense of the divine word-revelation – surely it behooves us heartily to thank Him.

1.4 And to Take Courage

But also to take courage. We are called upon to live out our lives in dark and terrifying times. From the time of the French Revolution on, our days have been filled with mounting confusion on all sides, with revolutions and acts of violence that seem only to increase in tempo, in range and in intensity. For more and more people life appears to lack any meaning. Even in the churches great numbers of people have accommodated themselves to secular ways of living and thinking, so that the power of Satan to deceive is mighty in the world. We can understand the words of Groen van Prinsterer, who said: "Modern society, with all its excellences, having fallen into bondage to the theory of unbelief, is increasingly being seduced into a *systematic denial of the living God.*"

Yet it is into *this* world that God entered in the person of His Son. The renewing, restoring, reconciling, the redeeming Word of God has come into our world and overcome the power of the deceiving Rebel and his destructive Revolution of Nihilism. Christ is Victor; He has made all things new; the forces of evil are done, even though they do not yet realize the fact. God has given us His Word not only to be our Light, but also to be our Comfort and Promise. The Word of God is for the renewing, for the healing, of the nations. And if we will but continue to believe – we are commanded, you know, to believe; it is not a matter of passively awaiting God's act – then Christ, who conquered at the summit, and has begun a good work in you, will perform it until the day of His coming in power and glory. This is always our only Comfort, both in life and in death.

If we will but continue to believe. But belief is obedience. "Faith," says our Groen Club syllabus, *The Bible and the Life of the Christian* (p. 77), "is obedience to the Revelation, a willing listening to the Word of God which results in acts of faith that relate to our time and situation" (Ps. 81:12-15). Faith which entails obedience is the victory that overcomes the world. Proverbs 3:5-6 can be translated, "Rely whole-heartedly on the One whose word is faithful... and He will clear the way for you." (See *Korte Verklaring, Spreuken I*, ad loc.) There are apparently irresistible roadblocks and impassable landslides which the "spiritual wickedness in high places" puts in our path. But God will clear the path and open a way. Our work is meaningful and will be effective, if we will but continue to believe.

Trust and obey, and God will pour out over your people here and over your life in Canada all the manifold benefits which derive from His cosmic redemption. Then we can confidently look for mountains to be removed, for spiritual hindrance in high places to be restrained, and we shall see contours and configurations of Christ's Kingdom of Righteousness appearing here and here and here in the land. The Lord has been pleased to begin the renewal of our whole life. Let us claim this Promise; let us believe; let us resist the devil, and he will flee from us. God's Word and it alone, but it assuredly, offers perspective for human life. Indeed, we can thank God and take courage.

1.5 Line of Reformation

We here are not the first in history to experience the reforming work of Christ, and part of our prophetic task is to take note of the "line of reformation" (a phrase I would wish to employ as a substitute for the, in my opinion, too narrow "line of orthodoxy" often referred to by theologians); we have the sacred obligation to declare openly where truly reformatorical activity has taken place and to call into loving remembrance those by whom the Spirit of Christ has wrought such reformation and (re)new(ed) obedience in times past.

As I was setting down these thoughts about what God has been doing in our midst in these last years I was strongly reminded of Prof. Veenhof's description of the time in which the Association for a really scripturally-directed philosophy was organized in Amsterdam (the mid-1930's). That low-point in Reformed life – for so it was – Veenhof describes as a heyday of criticism and relativism in theology and philosophy. The best spirits struggled against the flood; they felt it to be a question of life and death, for the church and for themselves. But in their work, in their study, they were unable to cope with the situation. The leaders did not fathom the danger; they were, though entirely unawares, deeply entangled themselves in the snares of all kinds of synthesis with (accommodation to) the ideas of their mortal enemies. A paralyzing defeatism took possession of large groups. A subtle psychologism destroyed in many the power and glory of a childlike faith... The ethicistic religiosity of the N.C.S.V. (Nederlandsche Christelijke Studenten Vereniging) infected the entire student world. A man was almost ashamed of being Reformed... Moreover, already an emerging bourgeois spirit, a spirit of rigidity, a growing spirit of worldliness in political activity in leading circles of the Reformed world had become offensive to men of a fine and keen spirit.

It was in the midst of this crisis, as Prof. Veenhof tells the story, that S. de Graaf, A. Janse, K. Schilder, Vollenhoven, Dooyeweerd and others appeared upon the scene. Veenhof writes of Vollenhoven and Dooyeweerd that the Kampen students heard them and were convinced by them in the student congresses held at Lunteren. "A new world," he recalls, "opened itself up to us... Everywhere God's Spirit was at work. Oh, no, nothing 'special' happened, actually. It was just that for a great many people the Scripture suddenly became clear. It was as though God's loving hand brushed away the dust that scholasticism and mysticism, pietism and every other kind of subjectivism and individualism had heaped upon His Word, in order that that Word might once again send forth its clear sound and shine forth as a lighthouse to give direction in a dark night."

1.6 Renewal of Dutch Student Life

From its beginning the renewal of Reformed student life in the Netherlands in the mid-1930's was simply a re-discovery, a recovery, of the Word of God, and therewith of true (i.e. scriptural) religion. It was not, in the first instance, the emergence of a particular philosophical system – what has come to be known in Dutch as the *Wijsbegeerte der Wetsidee* (Philosophy of the Law-Idea). Even the philosophers involved, as Christian men, recognized this and declared it forcefully. Professor Dooyeweerd has repeatedly said that not just a "new system" (burdened as such work always is with all the shortcomings and errors of human thinking) was his chief concern, but rather the foundation and root of scientific thought as such, in the light of what Scripture reveals concerning our life.

And on the occasion of the establishing of their Association for a scripturally-directed philosophy (1935) Professor Vollenhoven – who, thanks to the goodness of God, is here, participating in this Conference with us – spoke the following significant word which I have translated into English.

It is a glorious and blessed thing that brings us together here. It is not philosophy; for that is not the first thing in our life. It is rather the attachment to God's Word, because we have learned by grace to wish to live only out of the Christ, and religion, as a matter of the heart, has become the root-center of our life in its totality; because we have learned that only in attending to the commandments of the Lord are peace and life to be found, not only for the individual, but, to be sure, also for all those associations of life in which we find ourselves. This is why philosophy does not occupy the first place here. It has never held that position in our circles, and if the Association which we now propose to erect remains faithful to its task it will not be its fault if philosophy should ever become the prime consideration. We wish only to take that which is the main thing seriously in the philosophical work that we do... That is something we badly need; for the philosophy that is current knows nothing of all this that is so dear to us: nothing of God if you understand by that the God of the Scriptures; nothing of a heart that can find rest only in Him; nothing of a world-history that is bound up with the first and the second Adam; even very little of any difference between the spheres, the distinguishing of which in the practice of life proves to be so very essential.

1.7 Our Renewal: "Christelijk Studeren"

As it was among those Dutch students of the mid-1930's, so it has been with us here at Unionville. As persons and as students we have been brought back to the Word of God. Our chief concern here has been to understand better how that Word gives us direction in our studies. I am sure that I can say that it is the fervent wish, not only of the leaders of these Conferences, but also of the Board of the Association for Reformed Scientific Studies, which sponsors these Conferences, that the Word of God prevail and be operative in our lives as the central directing Power that it is. Perhaps I may be permitted here a

very brief excursus on this subject of *christelijk studeren*, studying in the Christian way. Very few, I believe – even among
those who sometimes talk nicely of its desirability – have really
seen what is involved, viz. the necessity of a scripturally-directed scholarly enterprise. Yet the growth of this insight is the very
heart of what we are trying to accomplish in these Conferences.
It is not true, as is frequently alleged, unfortunately, even by
many men of Reformation connections in our time, that the
Word of God has to do only with persons but not with the
subject matter of the sciences. When I here speak of *christelijk
studeren* I mean studying in the light of God's Word. I mean
that the divine Word illumines us as to the first or principial formulations of the several sciences. For when God's Word
takes hold of our hearts and reveals to us the central religious
character of our full selfhood, reveals to us thus that our whole
life is religion – see the lectures of last year – we at once begin
to be aware (unless powerful historical traditions blind us) of
the bearing of such word-revelation upon the problematics of
the several sciences as well as upon the manner in which we
organize our life of practice.

Let me – for this is only a brief excursus – take an example from the science of psychology. Psychology studies, among
other things, our sense-perception. In that connection we must
ask ourselves whether it is the "eye" that sees, or the I. And if
the latter, whether that I is the "rational soul" of Greek and
western intellectualistic philosophy or the religious self that the
Word of God reveals us to be. Accepting the light of the Word
about our central selfhood, we are given insight into what
some contemporary psychologists speak of as repressive or dis-
tortional perception, by which they mean that the perceiving

subject represses, delays or distorts his percept of something so that he will not see the thing (as it is). One well-known American psychologist introduces in this connection the "concept of perceptual defense".

The Word of God speaks of those who "hold down the truth in their unrighteousness" (Rom. 1:18) – in self-defense, of course – and if this rebellious religious act (of withstanding the powerful Truth of God's creation-revelation) is central to our selfhood, then in the psychical life of perception (which is one moment or aspect of our creaturely experience) we should find this central or total religious repression expressed in a psychical way, just as in logical investigations into the forming of our logical concepts we should find the same central religious man busy repressing the Truth in a logical way, e.g. in his substituting for the religious man of the Word of God the religiously distorted concept of "rational soul". The forming of this "logical" concept betrays the "direction" of apostate religion; for it expresses man's supposed substantial independence of God; its erroneous character cannot be explained in the purely logical way, i.e. in terms solely of the violation of logical laws.

Only in the light of the central thrust of scriptural revelation as to the religious nature of reality, i.e. that total man responds in a position of responsibility or Office to a world-order which is wholly *revelational*, and that this human response is either a newly learned obedience-in-principle (hampered by much sinful disobedience) or a rebellious disobedience (the latter limited in execution by God's sovereign maintaining of His law), are we able to discern (prophetically!) the falsity of traditional views of perception and to liberate ourselves from their grip so as to be directed in our formulation of the problems of the special sciences by the central revelational thrust of the Word of God.

This is what I mean by *christelijk studeren*, and at once it becomes clear how superficial it is to say that Christianity concerns persons but not the subject-matter of the several sciences. For what, after all, is the psychologist dealing with in his science if not the "seeing" of the see-er, if not just the *person* in the psychical moment of his selfhood? But if the Word of God reveals the person to himself (e.g. what it is to be a person), then this revelation has psychological, logical, and other implications. After all, it is *I* who perceive, *I* who logically form concepts, etc.

Nor ought we to forget that more traditional psychologies and logics have been "directed" by other (apostate) religious views of total man, e.g. naturalism, or Greek intellectualism, the latter, in one of its interpretations, in the Aristotelian hylomorphistic form mediated by Thomas Aquinas and contemporary neo-Thomist psychology and logic. There is no pure psychology, no pure logic, or pure any other science.

1.8 Purpose of Our Conferences

It is this idea of studying in the light of the Word of God that dominates our conferences here. It is this that we wish to bring to our students in Canada. This is not the same as to say that our intention is to have the *Wijsbegeerte der Wetsidee* govern these conferences. The *Wijsbegeerte der Wetsidee* movement has been and remains a powerful stimulus to study of the kind we wish to promote, perhaps the most powerful single stimulus, and it has profoundly influenced me and others who have spoken or are speaking here. But I can assure you that the idea of a narrow and sectarian binding to the special views of any man or any particular group of men is thoroughly repulsive to my Christian consciousness, and should be, I think, to every Christian consciousness. Though our conference speakers may often be associated more or less closely with *Wijsbegeerte der Wetsidee* circles, I can assure you that they are chosen for these conferences not because they belong to such circles but because we believe they can help us in learning to study by the light of God's Word.

It is important to remember – what we have already seen – that the founders of the *Wijsbegeerte der Wetsidee* movement themselves recognize only one bond, the attachment to the Word of God. For them, as for us, a Christian scientific enterprise is one that is materially, i.e. really, scripture-directed. Theoretical studies, both for them and for us, must appear in the figure of servant, – servant of Jesus Christ. Actually, the *Wijsbegeerte der Wetsidee* has no basis of its own devising, no sectarian foundation, nothing of human construction that is sure (Dutch: "vast") in itself, from which one would be obliged to conclude to something or other. Its leaders have constantly warned against the always present danger of party-formation. It does not canonize its philosophical articulations, but demands of any philosophizing of man that it be directed by the central word-revelation of God.

To see all our life, including our theoretical studies, as religion, i.e. as single-hearted service of God by man in his threefold office as God's vice-gerent in the world, subject to the all-encompassing and life-sustaining Law of God and in pursuance of the cultural mandate, – this is not some particular philosophical system, but only seeing our lives in the light of God's Word, by which same Gospel we are at the same time liberated from the fetters of the false Greek-western view of science as an autonomous rational enterprise of something called Mind or Intellect or Reason, something that is thus itself not just a function of the religious self which the Word of God reveals us men to be, but an independent substance.

In the last decades, some awareness of these things has been dawning in our too Greek-trained minds. Emil Brunner speaks of it, for example, in his book *Der Mensch im Widerspruch* (Ch. 9: Die Einheit der Person und Ihr Zerfall; Ch. 16: Seele und Leib), though other emphases of this book are not to be recommended. The best single book for you to read in this connection is perhaps Prof. G. C. Berkouwer's *De Mens Het Beeld Gods*, announced in an English translation to be published by Eerdmans in the spring of 1962 as *Man the Image of God*.

1.9 Biblical Basis of Unionville

The A.R.S.S. and these Unionville Conferences acknowledge no narrower basis than the Word of God. (See the Basis article – article II – of our Constitution.) Scripture is as broad as the Truth. *But Scripture is not "broad" in the sense of "vague." It is definite and decisive.* It will not allow, for instance, any view of man and all his activities which is not centered in the fundamental religious relation to God. It rejects any attempt to accommodate (synthesize) revelational Light and such apostate-religious principles of structurating our experience as that man just naturally comes to know the Truth because he is there, a rational being amidst a world of rationable entities (i.e. things the meaning of which can be grasped just by the penetration of rational analysis). The A.R.S.S. wishes to stand on the Word of God, also when that Word is decisive. We have formulated a confessional statement of the biblical perspective, which appears as article III (Educational Creed) of the recently published A.R.S.S. Constitution. We believe that all who, with us, desire that their lives be directed radically (from the root) by that Word, will come and take their stand with us on this North American continent. We invite all, whether Dutch immigrant or Canadian or American or whatever, who believe as we do to join with us in our effort to give our students a biblically-directed program of higher studies. Is this narrow or sectarian? The one who says so must mean by those nasty words what we mean by being truly ecumenical. For the Word of God alone, in its radical and integral Power, can destroy the party differences and one-sided commitments that arise among men when they do not submit to the Authority of that Word; and it alone has the Power to unite our hearts in a common confession of the Truth. This is the basis of genuine ecumenicity. In a very meaningful sense, we can claim that these Unionville Conferences are laying the solid basis for a truly ecumenical movement. More than Dutch immigrants or members of the Christian Reformed Church come here! Under God's indispensable blessing the influence of these Conferences is bound to grow.

1.10 Educational Creed Biblical

I am, of course, aware that it has even been suggested that our creedal statement or educational confession of faith (article III) is inspired by the *Wijsbegeerte der Wetsidee*. If there is any truth in this suggestion it is that the recovery of a proper (i.e. scriptural) understanding of the Word of God and the place it sovereignly demands for itself in our life, which led to the development of the *Wijsbegeerte der Wetsidee* in the first place, is also to be found in our Credo. Such religious awareness, however, is not the same as a philosophical system of thought. It is rather, we believe, God's gracious work of reformation, His turning of our hearts to hear Him in His Word and to do His will in the world. We publish our Credo as a statement of the sense of Scripture for the work we have to do.

There are those who will say that our rejection of synthesis-thought is proof that we are just a private *Wijsbegeerte der Wetsidee* movement. That would then make a man like Richard R. Niebuhr of Harvard Divinity School to be a *Wijsbegeerte der Wetsidee* man; for he writes in his book *Resurrection and Historical Reason* (p. 111) of a dilemma's developing in Bultmann's thought because he tries to "synthesize biblical categories with his Kantian and existentialist motifs". But such a conclusion is obviously ridiculous. The question here is whether what we mean by synthesis and our rejection of it is a *Wijsbegeerte der Wetsidee* notion or a scriptural idea to which the *Wijsbegeerte der Wetsidee* movement, among others, has given pregnant expression in our time. We believe the idea to be scriptural, and on this scriptural basis, formulated in our Credo, we stand resolute.

1.11 Discussion of Credo Invited

It would be better if our critics, instead of boxing with shadows, would make clear what they think is not scriptural in our Credo. That would serve to advance discussion and promote a clarification of issues. Merely to go on saying that our creed is too narrow and sectarian, that it is the *Wijsbegeerte der Wetsidee* (while it certainly and clearly is no philosophy at all), without taking us seriously as confessors of the Word of God and without responsibly pointing out to us where or how we are narrower than Scripture, – this is, to be sure, the easiest thing in the world to do (it can be done from a rocking chair), and it may serve to confuse some who do not stop to think and to keep such from sharing in our blessedness here (for my use of 'blessedness' here see *Christian Perspectives*, 1961, p. 12 bottom, and *Christian Perspectives*, 1962, p. 145 (end), 146), but it is not helpful.

Meanwhile, our young student generation has had a couple of years to sample what is offered here at Unionville. They know that what we are giving them meets their deepest needs as Christian students and provides them with real help in their student lives. They are also beginning to realize how rare and costly and highly to be prized such help is in this world. They sense the deep religious significance, for them and for this continent, of the work that is being done here. They have repeatedly and exuberantly demonstrated to us how they feel about it, and they will not be turned aside by empty and formal charges. They have tasted the meat. The product recommends itself. We might, all of us, instead of playing with names, better judge the Unionville Conferences and the A.R.S.S. by the *work that is being done*. Does it help us and bring us farther? If so, let us thank God and take courage. The Word of God provides perspective and the promise of fulfillment!

1.12 Special Introduction: The Present Lectures

And now at this our third Conference I propose to deliver three lectures on the subject: SCRIPTURAL RELIGION AND POLITICAL TASK. In one sense these lectures have been on my mind from the first. Yet they could not profitably have been given until now. For they do not just introduce one more topic, another more or less discrete unit, the third of three, so to speak. While this third series of lectures will, I trust, be sufficiently clear and meaningful to those of you who may be among us here for the first time, and also to those who may happen first upon the book in which they will have found lodgment, they do nevertheless presuppose all that I have been saying to you here in the past two years, and can properly be understood only in the light of the entire discussion. For they constitute part of an unfolding program. The three series, taken together, exhibit a dynamic development. I say this here at the outset in order to call your attention once again to the glorious fact that when the Word of God is acknowledged for what it is, *it leads to something*. We begin to get somewhere. We experience that the Word of God does indeed direct our "goings."

This is what is so very exhilarating about the work we are doing together in these Unionville Conferences. From a central religious reawakening there is emerging among us a gradually unfolding insight. We are acquiring a steadily deepening insight into the nature of the Word of God as in very fact the directing Principle of our entire life-dynamics, and therewith also (seen from the other side) of our life as radically and integrally scripture-directed. From year to year there has come a development in this insight. This year my lectures represent an effort to bring to articulation out of this insight that we have been gaining in the two previous years a scriptural position for one aspect of our heart-service of God, the political aspect. In the political area this is what Christians need most: the working out or articulation of this *central religious knowledge* for our political life. Hence, the title of these lectures: Scriptural Religion and Political Task.

1.13 Truth and Our Method of Working

By working in this way, I mean to protest, first in general, against much that takes place in educational circles today, unfortunately even in Christian educational circles. All too frequently, it appears to me, we are occupied with small so-called "units" of learning. The school year is being divided into increasingly smaller units of time. The various "units" of learning are treated as more or less discrete: the pupil or student learns one unit, is tested on it, and then goes on to the next. Behind this procedure, I take it, is the idea that truth is a matter of correct descriptions of limited states of affairs which are capable of being considered one by one. I do not believe that there is wisdom in this, and my belief derives from the integral nature of the Word of God and of the Order of Creation it reveals to us.

Undoubtedly, there is such a thing as descriptions of limited states of affairs. However, we ought not to equate such descriptions with the Truth. I believe we may assume of the Devil that he is acquainted with many more states of affairs than we are; yet Christ says that there is no truth in him (Jn. 8:44). To know the Truth is to acknowledge with the heart the true Order or Structure of God's creation taken as a totality or whole (Ps. 119:29, 30), to know (with the heart) that God is

God and man His creature and servant (in Adam or in Christ), to see that Christ's Kingdom of Righteousness is co-extensive with the restoration of all things to the Father and that therefore there cannot be, for instance, a "natural" scientific or political life that is not subject to the gospel call to repentance and a wholehearted life of obedient thanksgiving in faith. To be in the Truth, according to Scripture, is to be in Christ, Who is the Truth (I Jn. 5:20, etc.). In Him we know the Truth. "By his knowledge shall my righteous servant justify many," (Isa. 53:11; cf. Isa. 11:2. Read the *Korte Verklaring* at these places). The active and powerful Word of God brings home to our hearts the Truth of the central and all-encompassing reality of Christ's Kingdom of Righteousness, i.e. the Kingdom where everything is right with respect to the demands of the Law-order of God's creation-will (including sphere-sovereignty). The Devil did not remain in this Truth, but imagined to himself a world in which the relations were (are) otherwise. He is the father of lies; the Lie is of his very nature. (Read on this the instructive paragraphs of Dr. A. de Bondt's book, *De Satan*, pp. 137-142.)

1.14 Nature of Word of God and the Truth

As the Truth, the Word of God is not just a large collection of words, to be considered piece by piece by theologians or anybody else, but something much deeper, viz. the illumining, driving, directing Principle of our whole life. For this reason in the introductory section to my very first lecture here in 1959, which was printed in *Christian Perspectives*, 1960 as a separate chapter (and which I urge you now to re-read), I pointed out that THE question before us here in Canada is the relation of the Word of God to our life-in-the-world, and I ended those remarks, you will recall, by saying that the kind of Canadian society and culture that will emerge will basically depend upon the answer the Reformation youth of Canada give to this question. I added that the answer that is to be given will itself depend on *what the Word of God actually is*. Right at this central point vast confusion and misunderstanding reign because in the course of history men have accommodated Scripture's revelation about its own nature and place or role in our lives to their inherited (Greek) intellectualistic ways of thinking. Hence, scholasticism, with the ensuing and likewise distorted reaction of pietism.

In my second chapter (still the first delivered lecture of 1959) I therefore addressed myself more particularly to this question as to the nature of the Word of God and its role in our life. We saw that the Word of God is one Word of divine POWER by which God sovereignly opens our hearts to see our human situation in the framework of the whole of reality, the POWER that works in us an existential (not: existentialistic) awareness of the integral creation-order and, within that, of the radical Fall in Adam and equally radical Restoration in Christ, the second Adam. As for man, the whole of man, in all his temporal aspects and relations, is, through this powerful Word of God, integrally directed in the religious center of his being towards God, and is there concentrated on that whole-hearted service which is the fulfilling of the Law.

1.15 Life Is Religion

Thus we arrived at the insight that our whole life is religion. And that not only for Christian believers (true religion), but also for unbelievers. For unbelief is not described in Scripture as absence of belief, but as mis-directed belief. Religion, we saw, is man's ineradicable situation: he has been created "before God" (*coram Deo*) and must render an account of his doings and ways. It is the role of the Word that comes from God to illumine our hearts and direct our goings. But, likewise, men who lack this Light and Direction are prompted, by reason of their (now perverted) religious nature to do for themselves what that Word of God ought to do for them. Man acts in this religious way of demanding the full sense of things because of his having been created by God a religious being. He cannot escape his nature. Man wants to know the Truth, and the Truth is not a lot of separate pieces of knowledge that can be arrived at analytically. As a religious being man does not just analyze limited states of affairs that are immediately present(ed) to him. He orders or places or locates them, gives them a meaningful setting. As Prof. Van Riessen was saying this morning, fallen man, being a religious being (who must have a Word that reveals the Order or Structure of things), never just "accepts the facts," but rather invents, finds a way to put the facts so that he will be safe without God. In this way apostate man appropriates to his own heathen pistical phantasy the role that the Word of God really has, and thus from the beginning places himself in a world where the relations are (imagined) other than they really are. He lives in the Lie. *Human analysis always takes place within the context of the Lie or of the Truth.*

A knowledge of these things ought to affect the way we go about our studies. That is why, in my first set of Unionville lectures, instead of dealing with some *particular* problem or other I attempted something that for me was difficult to execute and for my hearers and readers probably even more difficult to get the hang of, at least in a first encounter, viz. to bring before us something of the *wholeness* of human life and experience *in the light of the Word of God.*

1.16 Last Year's Lectures

Last year I returned to this same central area in order to drive home even more emphatically the role of the Word of God as the directing Principle of our life. Referring to 1 Peter 1:23, I spoke of the divine Word as the starting-point of our (newly generated) life, a starting-point which at the same time determines the direction of that life's future course. Human life, if it is to have a firm direction, always requires a living faith, and the fundamental debate of our time is one about which faith – whether faith is recognized as such or not makes no difference here – is to direct our goings by taking possession of the "beginnings" of our lives, viz. our hearts.

In my first lecture last year I made an effort to elucidate the peculiar faith of modern times that is known as scientism, the belief in science as the avenue of revelation of the Truth, and at the same time to show that the scientistic attitude can maintain its hold on men's hearts only where men continue to fail to note something of the structure of the creation, viz. the presence of the *non*-scientific, which is also *pre*-scientific. I did this in order that we might the more clearly see the need of the Word of God to reveal to our hearts the Truth of our life in its radical (religious) unity, an insight which is simply indispensable to our understanding aright the place and nature of philosophy and the special sciences, but also to our becoming that perfect man of God, thoroughly furnished unto every good work (2 Tim. 3:17).

The thesis of my second lecture was that the concept of sphere-sovereignty (together with sphere-universality) gives accurate expression to the scriptural revelation about the structural "bouw" or make-up of the (religiously) integral creation. Here at once we see how the religious knowledge which the Word of God works in the heart of the believer gives first or principial direction as we are confronted with the rich diversity of life, and how thus we are at the same time delivered from the powerful hold that such traditional (also religious, but apostate-religious or synthetic) principles of structuration of our life as Matter and Mind, or Nature and Grace, Natural and Spiritual, or Secular and Sacred, have upon us.

I concluded last year that sphere-sovereignty is an eminently evangelical principle, being given with the Gospel itself, and that it is the badly needed corrective to the theologism and pietism that have contributed so much to the disintegration of the evangelical religion of Calvin and rendered the people of God impotent and directionless in our time. Finally, I expressed my agreement with Prof. Van Riessen's conviction that "at this point the decisive blow will be dealt in the struggle against totalitarianism and for a Christian society."

1.17 And Now Political Life

Only after all this, I am now suggesting, are we in a position to discuss profitably together the political task of Christians in our time and situation. If what we have said about the Word of God and about the role it demands for itself in our lives is true, then when we come to discuss the political aspect of our life in this world *we must begin with that Word of God*. And then with that Word in the sense in which we have understood it, as one Word, the one divine POWER that begets to new life, that illumines us integrally in our central religious selfhood (our heart), the Word which is the driving and directing Principle of our life.

1.18 Initial Obstacle

In emphasizing this point I am now meaning to protest, in particular, against the way in which discussions on our present topic usually are carried on among Christians. It is at this point, please note, right at the beginning of our discourse, that we are confronted with what in my opinion is our greatest single difficulty in getting such discussions off to a right and a fruitful start. We live so very much in terms of the immediacies of this world. Do we not see it all about us? Also in our own lives? Indeed, where is there a place where it is not being done? Everybody begins in his thinking with the immediately surrounding situations, in connection with our present subject with immediate *political* situations, and wishes to know what decisions he must make as a Christian *within these situations*, within the present problematics. In the U.S.A., for instance, one asks whether as a Christian he is to attach himself to the Republican or Democratic parties. One wants to know whether the one party or the other gives the best opportunity to do one's Christian duty. Usually this duty is conceived in some such direct way as "having a feeling for the lot of the common people," or some similar expression. An answer, if it is to be satisfactory to our somewhat impatient inquirer, must somehow fit into these immediately given situations or it is at once excluded as being – notice the language – too idealistic, not realistic enough. Genuine solutions, it is maintained, must fit the situations that have historically grown up; for the Christian, it is further asserted with some assurance, must live in the world. Here, without any doubt, we encounter one of the greatest obstacles to the proper and only possible development of really Christian theoretical and practical life on the North American continent.

Already in previous years I have uttered a warning here about the importance of beginnings, including the beginnings of our thought. You will recall that last year I referred to the statement made by Suzanne K. Langer in the first pages of her book, *Philosophy in a New Key*, that "the 'technique', or treatment, of a problem begins with its first expression as a question. The way a question is asked limits and disposes the ways in which any answer to it – right or wrong – may be given." Miss Langer concludes that "in our questions lie *our principles of analysis*, and our answers may express whatever those principles are able to yield."

This is a crucial point. The damage is done *in the beginning*. With regard to our political discussions, when we jump at once into an argument about details (for example, about whether we can agree with a particular expression of the Social Credit Party), when we demand direct answers to questions pressing hard upon us out of our immediate environment, then we are on the wrong road, we are *lost from the beginning*. That is because we have failed to recognize the nature and role of the Word of God. We are not to come out of our present lives in this world to the Word, there to find answers to particular problems our present lives present us with. That Word is the *directing Principle* of those very lives of ours. It is *in the beginning, at the beginning of our ways*, that the Word of God works its work in our hearts. If we begin from immediate situations we are lost from that moment on. For the Word of God came to bring all things back to a right relationship with the Father (Col. 1:19,20). There is a renewal of the problematics *from the beginning*.

In our sinful history things have gone wrong (developed in an unlawful way). To be concrete, last year we saw how men have blown up the life of the State to be the whole of our "natural" life at least. This reductionistic distortion, which is the environment in which our lives are lived, certainly ought not to be accepted as a starting-point for determining our political task as Christians. Neither ought we to begin our thinking about our political responsibility from the present *fact* that the only political directions in general available to us in the modern world are conservatism, liberalism, socialism, or communism. *The apostate religion of rebellious men has played its part in the forms that our modern life has taken on.* The Word of God, when it takes possession of our hearts, leads to reformation from the beginning, where the apostasy and the derailment began.

When, failing to understand the Word of God, we pay no attention to this renewal of the problematics from the beginning, but simply accept the surrounding situations and ways of thinking and of formulating the problems that have developed in the course of our (religiously directed) history, then we are already lost. Then we are not living (at least at this point) out of the Word of God. Then there exists no possibility for doing what nevertheless, according to the Law-Word of God, has to be done, the real task that the Christian has in political life as agent of Christ's reconciling work, empowered by the Spirit with the grace to effect a reformation *from the beginning*.

1.19 Living Out of Faith

In general, we may say that the Christian who really knows what it means to live out of the Word of God can never approach any aspect of his life merely in terms of its immediacies. He lives by the Word, out of faith in that Word. To live out of such faith is to live at a distance. This is not at all to say that the Christian is not immediately involved in the affairs of this world. Indeed, he is. But it is to say that his involvement in the immediately given situation is not directed by that situation itself. The Christian is engaged with this world in the sense of being involved with it and concerned about it; he is not *engagé* in the contemporary sense of belongingness and togetherness or of solidarity, in the sense, namely, that his life arises *out of* the community life. His life is hid with Christ in God. In the immediately given situations his "goings" are directed not by the "facts" themselves, but by the authoritative Word that comes from outside those immediate facts, from God. The Christian is *in* the world, but not *of it*. To use a form of language that Toynbee has again made popular in our time, the Christian's life is characterized by "withdrawal" (out of the immediacies to hear with the heart the Word of God) and "return" (with a reforming insight, to give a true and sure direction in the immediacies). This, and not personal withdrawal from the problems and situations of our life, is what Guillaume Groen van Prinsterer meant by his winged word: *In ons isolement ligt onze kracht*, i.e. in our isolation or in the sureness of our "strange"

Principle of life lies our strength to work reformatorically, thus savingly, in a world which has lost its way. *Populo salus*. The life of faith is a *relevant* life just because it brings the working out of redemption, of renewal, of reformation in a derailed world which cannot recover the meaning of things.

A very simple illustration will suffice. When David was being pursued by King Saul in the wilderness, there came a day when, as it seemed, God had delivered Saul into the hands of David and his men. These latter were hidden in one of the many caves of the region when suddenly they noticed the approach of Saul's band of men. A short time later King Saul himself appeared in the entrance of that cave in which David had taken refuge. The king fell asleep. What now is the situation? What is the *fact* of this situation? What do the facts *say*? Surely the Lord has delivered Saul into David's hands? That is what the (immediate) facts say to some of David's warriors. But not to David! David has a Word from God. David knows that God has called Saul to a position of office, the office of King. Saul, the anointed, is not to be touched by men without a word from God, and that had not been given. No; the facts do not speak by themselves. David is directed, *in* the factual situation, by the Word that comes from *outside*. That Word makes it possible for David to "go" surely in the circumstances.

We seek thus an approach to the subject of our political task from out of the central, radical, and integral religious illumination that the Word of God works in our hearts. It is so very important to understand clearly at the outset what this means that I think it may be useful right here to contrast our approach to the political task with another frequently encountered among Christians.

1.20 Wrong Approaches

We have got to come to clarity at this point. That many Christians have approached our present subject in another way does not in itself mean that there is more than one legitimate Christian approach. The "other" way I am about to describe has confused and dangerously sidetracked many Christians who nevertheless wish to take God's Word seriously in their daily living. And it can also easily be shown to have arisen from a faulty understanding of the Word of God.

1.21 Imitation of Christ

I refer to the inclination of Christian people, when confronted with problems in daily living, to ask themselves the question: What would Jesus do? This approach is vividly illustrated, for example, in a book entitled *In His Steps, or What Would Jesus Do?* that was widely read when I was a child in the fundamentalist circles in which I grew up, and which, I saw recently, is still available in bookstores.

Now it certainly is true, as Prof. S. U. Zuidema too has pointed out in his brochure *De Christen en de Politiek* (Uitgave: Antirevolutionaire Partijstichting, Dr. Kuyperstraat, 's-Gravenhage), that there is an important element of truth hidden in this way of approaching the problem. In its deepest nature the Christian life is nothing other than the following of Christ, nothing other than walking in His footsteps. But this very "following of Christ," this "walking in His footsteps" must, of course, be understood aright, which means that *we have to understand it in the light of the integral sense of the Word of God.*

If one means that by observing (in the Gospels, chiefly) how Christ acted in various circumstances while He was here on earth we can gradually come to know how He would act in various concrete circumstances today, that person has clearly not grasped the nature of the Word of God. Our following of Christ is not to be, indeed it cannot be, an imitation of Christ in specific historical situations described in the Bible. We are not to try to imitate specific situations, but to apply the principles of the Word and to live in the light of the Word as *one* Word, as our directing Principle. Our following of Christ comes only after the completion of Christ's Mediatorial work and the pouring out of the Holy Spirit: after Calvary, after the resurrection, after the ascension, after Pentecost. To follow Christ aright we must first be engrafted into Christ by the Holy Spirit, Who continues to lead the Church into the Truth.

1.22 Biblicism

Very closely connected with this inclination to seek the solution of problems of practical life by asking, What would Jesus do?, is another practice, the wrongness of which deserves to be pointed out here. Sober reflection will frequently bring Christians to the realization that they really do not know, and cannot find out by studying His life on earth, what Jesus (!) would do in specific situations today. (It is quite impossible even to know what a recent prominent church leader might do in circumstances that arise within his church only a year or two after his death.) Imitating the example of Christ is in this sense rather impossible. For this and perhaps for other reasons, Christians frequently look in the Scriptures for verses and passages that have a more direct bearing on, say, political life. By putting such particular passages together, one would then come, supposedly, to a scriptural view about our political life.

This lifting of so-called "political texts" out of the Word of God is again the result of a faulty understanding of that Word. Scripture is not a collection of words, some of which have a political reference; it is one Word. The practice we are here discussing is very much like what happens when men attempt to take specific prescriptions about food out of the Mosaic legislation as norms to be followed for diet, or to regard the form of the state found in Israel and described in the Old Testament (theocracy) as the norm to be followed by Christians in influencing the political life of their day. This use of the Scripture we call biblicism, viz. the effort not so much to live in the light of the one word of God as integral directing Principle of our lives as to imitate specific situations or apply particular text directly, i.e. lifted out of the Word taken as a whole. That this biblicistic attitude towards the Word of God as confessedly the Guide of our lives has played a significant role in our American life, and that it is not the view of Calvin and Beza, for instance, can be seen in the article by the distinguished former historian of the Free University of Amsterdam, A. A. van Schelven, "Het Biblicisme der Puriteinen van Massachusetts" (esp. pp. 111-112, 134-136), in his book *Uit den Strijd der Geesten*. As van Schelven (and also Bohatec, *Calvins Lehre von Staat und Kirche*, 1937, p. 14f) has there made clear, the position of Calvin developed in *Institutes* IV, 20, 14ff. is the more significant in that the idea of imitation was in much favour all around him. For instance, Karlstadt said that we must follow the laws of Moses "explosis Romanis legibus" (i.e. and let the Roman law – of his time – go to blazes).

When we understand what the Word of God itself witnesses as to its nature and the role it demands for itself in our human life, it is simply not possible to think of imitating the example of Christ, or of imitating specific situations, or of making a selection of specific "political texts" out of the Scripture, in each case then adopting these *as such* as norms for our political attitudes and work. We understand what Jesus would do and what the following of Christ entails, and we understand so-called specific "political texts" of Scripture or political situations encountered there in the truly scriptural sense only when we see all of these *details* in the light of Scripture as a whole, – what we have spoken of as the *integral* sense or illumination of Scripture.

The Bible is not a book of instructions for the various sides of our life. It does not give directions, but Direction. It is central religious revelation about God, and man in his central relation to God in the midst of the creation-order. The Word of God is directive for all our "goings" just because it is this central revelation about the place and calling of man in the cosmos. I repeat in this connection what I have already said once this morning, that *Christians are desperately in need of a political articulation of the central religious knowledge we have in Jesus Christ.*

1.23 Theory and Practice

Such an approach will, for instance, keep us from falling into a way of thinking which, though it is very widespread even among Christians, is yet in direct conflict with that scriptural illumination. For many will say, when we turn, as we are now doing, to the subject of political life, that we are leaving the theoretical area of our previous discussions behind us to enter upon an area commonly designated "practical life" or the "world of practice," where in the practice of daily life an application supposedly is made of the insights provided by theory. But, though theory and practice are indeed two distinct things, we may not think of our entire life as divisible into just these two areas of theoretical and practical life. Men speak commonly not of practice and theory, but of theory and practice, and this usage betrays the inherent underlying belief that the guiding Light or directing Principle for our "life of practice" is to be sought in some supposed theoretical (i.e. beholding) Reason, so that we first "see" the Truth by theory and then carry out what we have there seen in that other part of our life, practice.

As we know, not any such Reason but the Word of God is our Light and directing Principle, and when God by His Word sovereignly takes possession of us in our hearts and thereby sets us in the Truth, then, as Prof. Van Riessen too was saying so beautifully earlier this morning, we "see" and we "walk." That is so wonderfully Old Testament. New Testament too, for that matter. However, this "seeing" is not some beholding on the part of some concretely existing rational Mind of things the essence of which is their rational penetrability, but is the religious seeing of man as the Word of God reveals him to be, a man created to be God's representative on earth, created to hear the Word of the living God and to do it.

We are here in the scriptural sphere of "hearing and doing," where "hearing" is very close to the "seeing," the "insight," the "understanding of the heart" that we have talked about previously. But it is very important to observe also that the "doing" referred to in this scriptural expression is not what in the Greek and modern way of thinking is commonly meant by "practical life," but rather includes both theory and practice. The idea of Scripture is that when the Word of God illumines our hearts we "see" or "hear," and thus know how we are to "go" both in our theoretical thinking and in what we ordinarily speak of as our practical conduct. Theory belongs to the "doing" part of the scriptural expression. Our thinking "acts" as well as our practical conduct constitute our life-expression. Our theory, too, is part of the obedience we have to render, part of our religious service of God. It is not some divine Oracle come to dwell in us. It is not the Law; it is subject to the Law. Both our theoretical "goings" and our practical "goings" are "walked" under the direction either of the Word of God or, in the case of unbelieving men, of what the rebellious imaginings of the disobedient heart conjure up to take the central religious role of directing Principle of life (as, e.g. Reason).

As you can see, here Scripture enables us to reform our concepts of "world of theory" and "world of practice" in the light of its central religious revelation about the nature of man and of the role of God's Word in man's life. Here is a beautiful example of the 'ordering' role of the Word that we have been discussing. Both theory and practice take on a new meaning because they assume a new position, with respect to each other, and with respect to the religious depth-dimension of man's life which Scripture reveals.

1.24 Reason for These Lectures Now

And now it will be clear why I have chosen for this third series of lectures at Unionville such a subject as political life. Together with the rest of the work that I have done here, and with the lectures I give at Calvin College, for instance in Logic and in Greek Philosophy, these lectures round off our first encounter with each other – for next summer I shall be absent in Europe – in which I have attempted to be suggestive as to how both the theoretical and the practical life of the Christian is, when it is right, scripture-directed. When either theory or patterns of practical behaviour do not develop out of the scriptural illumination of the heart, then, by reason of the ineradicable religious nature of man, they are misdirected from out of a repressing, distorting religious starting-point. Then Christians ought not to accept the problematics, but to reform them. This is possible because of the work that God's Word does *at the beginning*.

That, out of the whole world of practice, I specifically chose for these lectures the political area is not to suggest in any way that our attention can be withdrawn from other areas. Life is one. We experience that here in Canada daily. The Christian Labour Association of Canada discovers that if it is to make clear the Christian's task in labour it must tackle much more comprehensive questions than just labour. Mr. Bernard Zylstra pointed this out at the conclusion of the address he delivered to the Christian Labour Association at its 1960 National Convention under the title, *Challenge and Response*.

1.25 Importance of Political Life

Yet there can scarcely be anyone who would wish to dispute the importance, and even the *urgency*, of Christian reflection on the political task. For political life is concerned with the *direction taken in the life of the State*, and the State, though only an aspect of the Kingdom of God, is nevertheless invested with the power of the sword. It has, as Althusius remarks, a certain *"majestas."* This power was bestowed by God, but it can be used wrongly. How horrible, how much worse than nightmarish a misuse of this power can be will be remembered by all who lived through the recent period of Stalin and Hitler. The power of the sword is indeed something to be feared. It comes into your and my family life, into our church life (think of the *Afscheiding* of 1834); indeed, with its power of the sword the State enters all areas of life. And this power is used. It will be used responsibly or irresponsibly, obediently or disobediently, but *it will be used.* For it is part of the structure of the life God created. Thus, the *way* this power will be used, the *direction* the life of the State will take in our time, will depend on the nature of the political action that emerges in the State. In the making, the interpreting and the administering of laws, the direction of the State-life influences us all daily. This element of direction is simply the basic or central religious Drive that is at work in all human cultural life (since life is religion). Here we have one of the reasons why the subject of political action is so very important.

A second thing that makes it extremely important is that thing we took note of last year in our lecture on sphere-sovereignty, viz. that, outside the small and as yet largely uninfluential area of scripturally directed thought, human life and society have frequently come to be reduced largely to the forms of *state*-life, so that, seen from the opposite end, the State has become to be blown up, totalitarian-wise, to be the whole of our natural life organized in society. With so much of our life so utterly drawn into the patterns-of-functioning of state-life, it becomes very important that in our political thinking we come to grips with what the State ought really to be in our life.

1.26 Urgency of Political Reflection

There are, besides political life, of course, many other important matters that must be thought about. Yet all of us are coming to feel the urgency of ripe political reflection. In the last
months here in Canada, for instance, in connection with the
Christian Labour Association of Canada, you have witnessed a
number of events which reveal vividly enough the monolithic,
oppressively totalitarian character of modern secularistic liberalism. I refer to the Etobicoke janitors, the difficulties the
CLAC has with, for example, the Ontario Labour Relations
Board, etc. Though these events may not appear to be strictly
political or State matters, ultimately involved is the "arrangement" or "order" of society, the relation of State to Church, to
religion, to union, and, in particular, the question of the public
state-powers granted by governments to privately organized labour unions. This is, of course, nothing other than the general
question of sphere-sovereignty. But because of the totalitarian
tendency of political life (the levelling tendency that arises because there is no proper insight into the structure of our life
nor, as a consequence, into the nature of the various spheres
of action), only an understanding of this evangelical principle
can enable us to free ourselves from the totalitarian oppression
and to find the freedom of life in its manifold activities that
humanists too are really seeking, though blindly, and to do that
by coming to understand the government's positive task, but
also its inherent limits. The whole debate in the United States
about state aid to private schools, and, in general, about the
first article of the Bill of Rights of our Constitution, is of the

very same nature. And the same questions underly the startling phenomena of our time, socialism and communism.

To add to the urgency of the matter, there is in both the U.S.A. and here in Canada a certain political unrest. In Canada this has already given rise to the New Party, and Stanley Knowles writes that Canadians are sick of the old conservative and liberal parties and desire a change. In our time a fundamental realignment of political forces looms up as a real possibility. The new forms that could arise out of the present unrest might be determinative of our political life together for many long years to come. In a time that is so dreadfully serious, when the current of history picks up speed, should we not once again inquire into the Order of God? Now, indeed, is the time for us to consider our political task, and to be reminded that the Word of God directs also our political life-expression *from the beginning.*

1.27 Division of Material

This then is the reason why I am speaking to you on the subject: SCRIPTURAL RELIGION AND POLITICAL TASK. And in order to bring out still more the connection of these lectures with those of previous years I have decided to hark back to the arrangement of my first year's lectures, and to divide the material into THESIS, ANTITHESIS and SYNTHESIS. But now, in connection with the political insight we are here seeking, to add to each of these words a qualifying phrase, thus:

THESIS: its political articulation

ANTITHESIS: the forms of its political expression and their development in modern times

SYNTHESIS: its contemporary political expression

1.28 Thesis

In the remainder of this morning's lecture, therefore, I should like to direct your attention to *the political articulation of the THESIS*. It will help you if you will recall that by THESIS I mean God's original Truth, the Order or Structure *laid down* – that is the meaning of 'thesis' – in the Act of Creation, the *knowledge of which* is religiously worked in us when the Word of God, the Gospel of Jesus Christ (the Re-publication in the second representative or Office-bearing Man of that Order of Creation, centered in the covenantal life-fellowship of God and man), sovereignly takes possession of our hearts. You may refer for this to *Christian Perspectives*, 1960, p. 107, 110-111, 133, 134, 136.

In this light Christian political action can only be political action that is directed integrally by the hold that the Word of God as one Word and directing Principle has upon our hearts. In the time that remains I shall make an effort to suggest in what way the Word of God thus directs the beginnings of our political "walk."

1.29 Principled Politics

Our recovered insight into the Word of God as the authentic Principle to guide us in the whole of our life-walk liberates us, in principle, from the aimlessness, the apathy, the meaninglessness, – in short, from the *lostness* that characterizes so much of human life, including political life, in our time. The Word of God enables us to act with sureness, to act in an effective manner which is bound to prove wholesome or salutary

(Latin, *salus*, meaning "salvation") for human society. This is to say two things. First, that Christian political life is a matter of principle. It is principial politics, directed by a Principle, and not, as almost universally in the world round about, pragmatic-opportunistic.

Even our present pragmatic-opportunistic politics arises, as we shall see in the second lecture, from an earlier political activity which was directed by a principle. How could it be otherwise? Life is religion, and either the *sure* Word of God or else an unreliable imagined substitute is in that central and prior place of religion, directing our "goings" as Principium or Arche. In reality, all political activity is principial. The principle modern man had believed was unreliable, and the present pragmatic-opportunistic politics develops out of a *loss of faith in the ability of that principle to direct surely*. Hence, its aimlessness.

Second, it is to say that Christian political action is full of hope and joy. For our Principle is, as we have seen, the sure Word of God which has entered our life to accomplish that for which it was sent, the redemption of the world. The Word of God, as we have already said this morning, is not only our Light, by which we walk, but also our Comfort and Promise. It offers perspective for human life, also in its political aspect. It drives on to the Consummation of all things in Jesus Christ. Psalm 1 says of the man whose life is directed by the Law (Word) of God that "whatsoever he doeth shall prosper."

1.30 Politics, an Aspect of Our Religion

The living and powerful Word of God sets us in the Light of the Truth: it discloses to us that our life in its integral wholeness is religion. Christian political life is therefore an aspect of our single-hearted life-walk before God. But the Word of God does not merely reveal to us what our life is; by the grace of God it also begets us to new life. It saves us. That is, it makes life-service of God again a reality (in principle). The Word of God, and it alone, is the POWER that restores us to our (religious) place as MEN before God (as opposed, you will remember from last year, to "the scientific mind"), MEN of God, thoroughly furnished unto every (also political) good work. Our political life is properly seen only when it is viewed as one aspect of our whole-hearted *Gottesdienst*, which God Himself has given back to us in his Son.

Where in *political* life today do we find such MEN of God, who, in Christ, have been made to stand once again in their human Office before the face of God in order that they may survey the whole of the Order of Creation, knowing that everywhere in that vast creation-order their responsible task is to serve God faithfully, in accordance with His Law (e.g. sphere-sovereignty), in integrity or singleness of heart? Christian political life has need of such (politically minded) MEN of God. Out of our life together as Christians such MEN of God must come forth to assume their responsibilities in the *political* sector.

1.31 The Religious Antithesis Real Also Here

Of course, all political action is religion, though we may not overlook the difference between true (real) and false (imagined). Since all human life is lived out of the ineradicable and fundamental religious relation to God, all political life must express the belief of those who are engaged in it. This is true even where it is denied; its truth is its rootedness in the sureness of God's creation-ordinance. Thus the political life of mankind generally will disclose the same fundamental religious Splitness or Antithesis of direction that characterizes human life as a whole. In their faith, i.e. in their ultimate certainty, the "ways" of men diverge. This is the meaning of scriptural revelation. "Fortunate then," Prof. Mekkes once wrote, "is the land that knows how to maintain in the purest possible way, also in its politics, this fundamental and central diverging of the "ways" of men... For then the political life of a country also gives clear witness to the real meaning of human life. Where this is not the case" – since life is religion – "it is due to the fact that the universal Christian principle of life has been pushed onto the background in political life by other contrasts and divisions that in the life of humanity are only secondary" (Mekkes, art. "Christelijke Politiek", in *Antirevolutionaire Staatkunde*, Vol. 21 (1951), pp. 285-303).

In other words, that land is fortunate whose political divisions mirror the real, and not imaginary or secondary, differences in our human life. If religion is the real ultimate directive of all our life "issues," if it *really* determines men's views, then any attempt to hide this basic religious dividedness by saying, for example, that we are all born either little conservatives or little liberals (a la Gilbert and Sullivan), or that we are all either "bourgeois" or communist, or whatever the accepted disjunction, is actually equivalent to saying something that basically is not true. These are not the *significant* division in our life, and one is only deceiving himself who thinks and says so. Believing the Lie, one then is driven on to an increasingly distorted outlook on *what is really going on in life*. Our life is always principial, i.e. directed by a religious Principium. Where political life becomes genuinely principial, thus when men in politics are driven to state what ultimately moves them to the political work they undertake, the real religious dividedness of men's "ways" will appear more and more. And political life will become more lively.

Christian political life is an aspect of our religion, this latter being understood in the true sense that the Word of God has once again disclosed to us. It is very important therefore, again in this context, that we clearly distinguish the scriptural meaning of the Christian religion from a number of misunderstandings or perversions of it which have most unfortunately arisen in the course of the centuries to distract believers from their central and integral task in this world.

1.32 Christian Religion Not Theologism

The Christian religion is not properly understood when man's religious "hearing" of the Word of God in his heart has been narrowed down to mean a scientific theological effort to render the sense of Scripture in the manner of a rationally articulated statement. God's Word is, in the first sense, the powerful Word of Him with Whom we have to do, which, with all the sovereignty of Him Who addresses us in it, begets us to new life, illumines us in our hearts and directs our entire life-expression. It sets us in the (whole of the integral) Truth. This is our integral *life-experience* of the Truth even before we can analytically set it forth. This integral Truth is very much more than just the theological way of understanding it. It is, first, *directive*, and then of *all* our life-"goings" and not just the theoretical ones. Further, in the world of *science* (Wissenschaft) it is directive of all our theoretical articulation, from out of the wholeness of our pre-scientific experience, and not just of our formulation of *theological* propositions. The Christian religion is definitely not the formulation (and acceptance) of specifically theological propositions out of the Word of God written, which are then to be added to a body of (other kinds of scientific) knowledge that is arrived at by some other 'personal centre of experiencing' that is outside the ultimate religious situation and directedness of our lives (as e.g. Reason) and thus free of the reforming POWER of the enlightening Word of God upon our hearts. This scholastic or theologistic perversion of the Christian religion would allow most of our life in this world to be free of the reforming POWER of the divine Word, and thus ultimately requires that we abandon that view of the Word of God that the Word of God itself instilled in our hearts, viz. that it is the directing Principle of our life in its integrity. In such theologistic circles no need is felt for a Christian political action, except perhaps in the sense of dealing with certain "immediacies."

1.33 And Not Pietism

The Christian religion is not mysticism. It is not world-flight. Scriptural religion is not a matter of God and something called the "individual soul." In the first place, it is not a matter of soul as something separate. Paul writes (Rom. 12:1): "I beseech you therefore, brethren, by the mercies of God, that ye present your bodies a living, holy and God-pleasing sacrifice; this is your proper *Gottesdienst.*" In the second place, the Christian religion is not a matter of God and *individuals.* It is not asceticism; it is not monasticism. It is not individualistic pietism, which attempts to attach an "inner," "personal" piety to the "external" ways of living of the time and situation (typical accommodation or synthesis). There is no such "inner," or "personal" thing or place, (in) to which we may withdraw, there to abide in quiet rest, removed from the great Wrestling of spirits. In the Scripture, soul or heart is not such a "place apart"; it is the religious point of concentration of my life, where *I* face God, hear His Word, and from out of which I am *driven*, in the totality of my bodily life-expression, in all kinds of relations and associations with my fellow-men in the world, *in a certain direction, to work in the world.*

It needs special emphasis in our day that the Christian religion is not a matter of "saved individuals" going around exercising a wholesome "personal" influence from out of their supposed "inner" life in Christ while the so-called "outer" life, unreformed by the POWER of the Word of God, is permitted to go on in the accepted fashion of the time. Such a view is simply a subtle form of world-flight: our living in the world is left untouched here; there is only the influence of one *person* upon another *person*, as it is commonly said. But a human person, according to Scripture, is quite different from an "inner soul," conceived as something withdrawn, a thing apart. Scripture teaches that out of the inner man (heart or soul) come the "issues" of life. Religion in its antithetical structure is also in the world round about us, not just in men's "souls."

Communists would not have been able to sell to great masses of men their caricature of the Christian religion as "opium for the people" or "pie in the sky" if Christians, instead of giving themselves to such perversions and misunderstandings of the Christian religion as theologism, mysticism and pietism, had lived more by the integral Light of scriptural revelation.

Here at Unionville we know that according to Scripture *the Christian religion is the re-direction, in Christ, the second Adam, of the whole of mankind's life in the world*. In Christ, man is restored to his Office, his God-appointed and responsible Place as ready servant of God in the whole of the creation-order.

1.34 Scriptural Concept of Office

The scriptural concept of Office throws into relief two essential features of our Christian religion. It implies *an assignment in the world*, and it gives emphasis to the *corporative character* of the assignment.

1.35 Implies Task in the World

As we said last year, "office" implies the assigning of a task and the bestowing of a right to perform that task. Our salvation is not something a "separate soul" receives to enjoy somewhere up above the affairs of a supposedly "bodily" life; *it is something to be worked out in the concrete circumstances of our life in this world*. Communists, far from being in conflict with the Christian religion, are rather in possession of a "trace" of the Truth about our life when they feel earnestly the need of a salvation that is here and now. When we say that in Christ man is restored to his Office, we are saying that the whole religion, the whole life, of man is the responsible and integral performing of a God-assigned task in the world, a performance stemming from the "hearing" of the divine Word and issuing in both theoretical and practical "acts" of loving obedience. By this obedience our life – very concretely – comes to be saved. This salvation-by-obedience of our life as a whole, of course, involves the salvation-by-obedience of our life in its political aspect. Thus is guaranteed the *reality* of a Christian political task. This means that an integrally Christian man cannot ignore the political side of his life-task, and, further, that he has to see this political task not as a separate activity-in-itself – as though political "life" were concrete life – but always as an integral part of his (religious) life-walk before God. Life is religion. In this light we arrive at a true insight into the nature of the Christian political task.

1.36 Excludes Individualism

At the same time, the scriptural concept of Office excludes all forms of individualism and points up the corporative character of the Christian religion. Not in ourselves, as individuals, but only *in Christ*, as members, along with all our fellow-believers, of the Body of which He is the Head, are we restored to our task in the world. Remember what I said the first year (*Christian Perspectives*, 1960, p. 156f.): when, like Adam, Christ was tempted of Satan in the wilderness, the heart of the man Christ was held in the grip of the Truth, and He gave to each of Satan's tempting words the integral answer of the Truth. Christ saved the Office of man, and to Him is given all authority. He has the Office, and we only in Him. Though the Spirit of God regenerates the hearts of individual men, it is not correct to say that God's redemption of the world in Christ is the saving of individual souls. God has established in His Son a second responsible man-in-office, a second Head of the race. It is the work of the Spirit of Christ to unite us men to this our Head. Christ having stood in the Truth, all His children who are thus united to His life in the one Body are also given insight into the Truth. "By his knowledge shall my righteous servant justify many." In this commonly shared insight into the Truth the new and only genuine Community is born, with a common insight, thus also, into its task in the world.

Actually, men always are drawn together in communities, and these communities are always faith-communities, rooted in a common (religious) insight. That is why governments, for one thing, seek to awaken in their citizens a religious attitude of commitment (patriotism). Individualism is not a correct theory about man's life; it is always false, always in conflict with reality. Even where men are busy theoretically and practically proclaiming individualism their very actions belie them. Here we have the religious reality behind man's constantly renewed search for genuine community, whether on the local, the national or the international level, but likewise – in the light of the reality of the Antithesis or Split in the religious rootedness of mankind – the reason for the disillusionment and failure in which all efforts to build a community of mankind outside of the Body of Christ are bound to end. Scripture gives us no hope for such endeavours. When Christ returns, His Kingdom will visibly and universally be established, but He must first put down every enemy. Mankind does not of itself come to one world! (This does not mean that we cannot have a world organization to discuss and regulate our life *in the light of our differences*. This is quite a different thing. World organization can mean more than one thing, and can be built in more than one way.)

The Christian religion is the glorious proclamation (of God's grace) that the life of mankind has been re-directed to God in its new Head. Humanity and humanity's life-in-the-world (i.e. men *together*, corporatively, in the totality of their bodily life-expression, in all the relationships and ways of association the creation-ordinance makes possible) has been saved, is being saved and will be saved, in Christ. *Together*, as organs or instruments of the Body, the new Community that lives in the Light of the Truth, we who are in Christ are to take up our human task in the world. Thus also the political (aspect) task. This latter, too, is part of our common *confession* to the world.

Accordingly, the Christian political task is not something individual Christians can take up according to their individual insights. It is not something that we may feel for or not feel for, take or leave as we please, depending on whether we "happen" to have, or to think that we have, some more developed political interest or ability (in Dutch: *een knobbel*). For example, we may not say, as so many "intellectuals" in Germany used to do, that we will leave politics to the politicians and the soldiers (see last year's lectures). The Christian political task is part of the divine Assignment, part of the cultural mandate to the human race; but it is a task given to God's people, the renewed humanity, to accomplish together out of their knowledge, in Christ, of the Truth. It is an aspect of our building together the Genuine Community or Kingdom that is sure to destroy all those other kingdoms ("communities") and to endure forever.

1.37 Difference Between Individualism and Particularization of Office

We do it together. That is not to say that all are to participate in the political task in the same way or to the same degree. But this is not the same as to say that some Christians are just naturally politically minded and others not, and that we must leave such things to the experts. We have here to do with the particularization of office (*ambtsverbijzondering*) in the one Body, where all have a responsibility conjointly with the rest. We cannot *leave* our task to others.

1.38 Office Means Service and Administration

Last year we saw that Office includes both service (*dienen*) and administration (*bedienen*). Office means, in the first place, service of God. But, second, it means the administration, in His name, of the world, an administering of God's love and solicitude to the creature (*Christian Perspectives*, 1961, p. 68). A brief remark about each of these aspects of Office as they bear on our present subject.

1.39 Christian Politics as Service of God

The Christian political task is first of all service of God. It is that as part of our whole religion. When we assume our human task, we place ourselves under the sovereignty of God and inquire as to His ordinances and commandments. We begin with the confession: the Lord reigns! Not we, not Chance or Necessity, not the Zeitgeist or Progress, but the Lord reigns. Therefore, we must obey Him. His glory is our first concern.

1.40 Divine Law-Structure

We saw last year how intimately the principle of sphere-sovereignty is bound up with the creation-ordinance of God. Sphere-sovereignty is not an intellectual construct of men in the first place. It becomes that when we begin to think about it, but first it is a *given* of the Word of God, *revelation* about the structure of the world and of our life in it. Thus it is revelation about the Lord's will, to which we have to subject ourselves. For the political aspect of our task this means that we have to discover what, in the light of the reality of sphere-sovereignty, God *intends the State to be*. In the course of history, the State emerges in a variety of forms (the several states) as a result of the positivizing activity of men. But this human work is religious work, and as such is subject to the Norm for all human action, the Will of the sovereign God. If we are to judge the several historical forms the State has assumed – and this belongs to the prophetic aspect of our human Office or Task – then we must have principial illumination as to the structure of the State. The Christian may not accept as norm anything other than what God has ordained for the peculiar "life" of the State. Accordingly, the Christian political task is to come to a recognition of that specific aspect of authority which God in His creation-ordinance delegated to the State.

Within the Body of Christ there must thus come basic reflection about the typical structure of the State, its peculiar nature and specific task. In the light of our developing understanding of the principle of sphere-sovereignty the Christian Body must arrive at a confession (our human response to God's revelation) about the limits, but also about the (limited) positive task of the State. Especially, the modally qualified task of the State must become clear.

1.41 Illustration of Modal Qualification

This last point can be clarified with the help of a simple illustration. "State" is like "Stock Market." I point to a certain building and say, "There you have the Stock Market." But it is true only in a certain sense that in that building we shall find what we call the Stock Market. Much more activity than can properly be spoken of as Stock Market is going on there. Here, for instance, stands a man whose eyes are frequently being diverted to the beautiful young lady in the balcony. There stands another, who, "between the acts," is thinking over that difficult section on the *That Which Is* of Parmenides in the book on Greek Philosophy he was reading the night before. And over there is another man whose thoughts are constantly returning to ways in which he can better fulfill his fatherly responsibilities to his growing children. The concrete life there on the floor of what we customarily speak of as the Stock Market is the whole range of human life, which concretely can only properly be described as religion. The words "Stock Market" require some abstracting from this full range of life-activity; they refer to a particular kind (mode) of law-structure which somehow organizes what is typically going on there. And so it is also with "State." Not everything going on in the Parliament or the Congress is "State"-life. Nor is everything a particular state does typical "State"-life. In what, precisely, does "State"-life consist? We must come to such a *modal* delimiting of the State's task.

1.42 Present Situation

I should not like to leave the impression that Christians have always had such wisdom in their possession. The power of the synthetical attitude (see the third of these lectures) has led many Christians, even of the Protestant Reformation, to attempt to understand our life, for example, in terms of Nature (State) and Grace (Church), so that very little progress could be made towards a proper delimitation of the tasks of either Church or State. Where, however, in more recent years the principle of sphere-sovereignty has increasingly been understood, some development along this line has taken place. It is here that we should begin. Let me mention, in particular: (1) Dooyeweerd, *De Christelijke Staatsidee*, and the very important relevant sections of Vol. III of his (thus far) main work, *A New Critique of Theoretical Thought*; (2) K. Groen, "Kriterium en Begrenzing der Staatstaak," five articles in *Patrimonium*, Vol. 66 (1955), April, May and June. Also art. Dooyeweerd, in *Antirevolutionaire Staatkunde*, Vol. XXII (1952), p. 65ff.

In this way the Christian political task involves calling a halt to the expansionist (totalitarian) politics that emerge in the life of the State where men who do not live by the light of the Word of God and have lost almost all sense of sphere-sovereignty find themselves with a levelled (Dutch: *genivelleerde*) view of State and society that knows no limits ordained from above, but only more or less arbitrary limits put by the popular will or the ruler. Here is a problem in the modern world which is overcome in the Christian religion. In the modern political mind, who is there to call the State to (its) order? The meaning of Office in human life has largely been lost; every man carries the ultimate Light around within himself, in his Reason, and thus has an equal right with every other to say what the State shall do. Further, there is no recognition of divine ordinances. But in the light of scriptural revelation, Prof. Zuidema once wrote, who can better call the State to order than the man who knows himself called to order by the high God? Than the man who trembles before the sovereign Law-Word of God?

1.43 Christian Politics Not a Question of Details

The Christian political task is thus concerned with the *inner reformation* of political life itself as an aspect of the integral renewal of our whole life in obedience to the divine Word of Salvation. For this reason, it can never be thought of in terms of some one particular question, of this or that political issue or campaign plank. A Christian political program can never be a one-cause platform, such as: no booze, no prostitutes on our streets, no underworld connections, no weak money, no state-financed medical program for the less fortunately situated, no share the wealth plan, return of the gold standard, or whatever. Taken by themselves all such things have nothing at all to do with the Christian political task. For the same reason, a Christian political party would be a political party, not a workers' or intellectuals' or gentlemen's or farmers' party.

It is surprising how even in the Netherlands today many people feel that the Christian political parties, after a period of struggle against the threatening state socialism of Kuyper's time, have now only to orient themselves with respect to questions of detail. This, of course, is not true. We have already seen in this lecture that Truth is not a collection of disparate items, and it is really amazing to see how time after time, in all kinds of seemingly purely "practical" questions of detail, the very fundamentals of our society are involved. Yet a dangerous situation arises when people give credence to such a positivistic view. Then faiths are often taken for facts. At the present moment, for instance, Protestant Christians who are not aware of the principle of sphere-sovereignty, partly because of the long history of scholasticism even in the theory of Protestant scholars, are often inclined to accept *theories* about the relations existing between various sectors of our life as *simple facts* when in fact they are not un-principled facts at all, but views arising naturally out of the long scholastic tradition about the world-order that we know as Nature and Grace, out of such a theory about parts and whole, out of a typical Roman Catholic corporative idea of subsidiarity.

A former Dutch government minister who is a member of the Dutch Labour Party (Partij van de Arbeid), in a lecture to a political science class at Calvin College, gave the impression that the old view of religiously directed political party action was dying away in the Netherlands and that men in ever in-creasing measure were coming to see the wisdom of leaving the religious questions to the churches, thus allowing the po-litical parties to be free to deal with political questions. At the end of his lecture questions were solicited, and someone asked whether this solution he favoured was not itself a philosoph-ical-religious solution, arising from a certain view of the rela-tion between religion and political life. His answer was classic, something to remember always. He said simply, *"Dat is even een moeilijk probleem"*; in English, "Indeed, there is a bit of a difficulty there." Yes, indeed. But it is not *"even een moeilijk probleem."* Here is *the* problem. His "solution" allows for sepa-rate dealing with purely political problems because he believes that the various aspects of our bodily expression-life are not religiously directed from out the heart. The difficulty is that he would – in a totalitarian way – attempt to foist his particular religious faith on all his fellow-citizens *in the name of positive fact*. This question as to what a fact is, is just not that simple. Not everybody will accept this man's easy identification of his personal belief with "the facts"; others have another *belief.*

1.44 Nor of Christian Persons in Existing Positions

It will by now also have become clear why a Christian political action can never be simply a question of getting Christian persons into existing political positions. Unfortunately, many Christian people feel safe as soon as they see the same old political life carried on by Christian persons instead of by supposedly non-Christian persons. As we have seen, however, we cannot enter directly into "immediacies" because religion exists in all human cultural activity, in all the forms and organizations to which men have given positive form, in the course of affairs (*de gang van zaken*), and not only in the hearts of persons. We must discern the spirits or directions of all that cultural activity, distantiate ourselves from unbelief, and establish our goings by the light of the Word of God. Christian political life is not the accepted political life of the time done by Christian individuals; *it is doing the will of God from the heart in the political sector*, exercising our Office according to the will of the Sovereign as revealed in the Word of God.

1.45 Christian Politics a Following of Christ

In this we are "followers of Christ" in the scriptural sense of the term. Christ was the great *Ebed-Jahweh*, Servant of Jehovah. He came to do His Father's will, and to do nothing else than that. To stand faithful in the Office of man, to be servant of God in the whole of His Father's creation. The will of His Father, we read in Col. 1:19 – see the *Korte Verklaring* on this passage –, was through Him *to bring all things, whether in heaven or on earth, back to a right relation to the Father.* Everything that has become disrupted and distorted is to be brought back to a right relation to the Father, Who in the Creation of the world had established His Thesis or Truth and declared it to be *very good*. Here is the cosmic redemption of Christ, the *re-creation*, the bringing back of all things to the Law-demands of the creation-order. This is the coming of the Kingdom of Christ, the Kingdom of Righteousness (the righted Creation) which it is also our whole task in life to serve (Matt. 6:33). For Christ Himself pointed to the parallel between His own work and ours when He said, "As (the Father) hath sent me into the world, even so send I (you) into the world" (Jn. 17:18). Young people of the Reformation, when, in the midst of life, you suddenly come to ask yourselves, Who am I and why am I here? Remember that the Word of God gives a clear answer.

1.46 Christ's Unique Work as Mediator

Yet there lurks a great danger here. Christian political action *is not an imitation of Christ*. Like the whole of the Christian life of which it is an aspect, it is *a following of Christ*. But then a following of Christ *in the scriptural sense*. We are to follow Christ in His ready obedience to His Father's will. In Christ we are also agents of God's reconciling work of recreation in the world. But there is a part of the Colossians passage we have just quoted which was then omitted: "having made peace by the blood of His cross." We may not forget that our Lord had also to obey His Father's will in that wholly unique life-calling He had assumed, His mediatorial work. That was His task and His alone. In this Christ can be neither "imitated" nor followed. That way He had to go alone as the One who bore our sins and paid the price for us. Our following of Christ in the scriptural sense begins after this unique mediatorial work has been accomplished and the Spirit has united us to Christ. The disciples had to wait with their service at Jerusalem until the Spirit had been poured out upon them. Only then could they be sent out with power into the world. To talk of the Christian life as an imitation of Christ is a failure to realize the *uniqueness* of Christ's position as Mediator between God and men. Our following of Christ is not that, but consists in being baptized with the same Spirit and made willing likewise to do, in our place in Christ, the Father's will.

1.47 A Wrong Question

Christ's whole life on earth was, in a very real sense, the inimitable life of the Mediator. For that reason the question whether Christ participated in the political life of His day (asked, of course, in order to discover whether we Christians, by way of imitation, also have a political task) is from the outset a wrongly formulated question that a proper understanding of Scripture will not allow, and which, if it is taken seriously, can only evoke wrongly formulated answers. What we have to do is not to answer the question but to reject it. Christ came to save the world in its very foundations. Out of His unique mediatorial work and the founding work of the apostles a whole Christian life would develop. Then a gradual working out of the new Way, the new Life, an articulation of the Truth in the life of mankind on all its fronts would ensue. Now, in Christ, attached to His Body and in the power of the Spirit, we are constituted agents of God's reconciling work in the cosmos. This is our life-service, and to it, as an aspect, belongs our political service of God.

1.48 Christian Politics as Administration of World

Besides service, "Office" includes administration. Service of God and administration of the world are not two separable concrete things; they are two distinguishable aspects of our exercise of our Office. The Bible teaches clearly (in connection with the exodus of God's people from Egypt) that God is especially glorified in the redemption, in the proper administration, of His people. This involves first a special land (Palestine) and will finally require a new heaven and a new earth wherein dwelleth righteousness. Christ came to do the Father's will, but the will of God involved the administration of the creation in such a way as to bring everywhere a salutary (saving) acknowledgment of the Law-word of God. The whole creation is God's, is *really* subject to His Law, and any saving administration of it will itself be one of obedient subjection and will seek to bring a hearty acknowledgment of the Law everywhere. Here we are at a point to understand the scriptural meaning of love. Christian love involves the world and our fellow-man in a very real way, but in such a way as to bring them into subjection to the life-constituting and life-preserving Law of God. There is no genuine love of the neighbor that is not at the same time and in the first place a whole-hearted love of God Who has revealed Himself in His Law-word. Much of the "I – Thou" talk of our time is empty talk because the "thou" is just as lost as the "I," both must "be" in a proper relation to the God Who is revealed in His authoritative Word.

The Christian political task is to bring to the world, in the political way and for the political side of its life, the blessing of Christ's redemptive concern for the world. It is a task directed to human society in the world. It is genuinely Christian and meaningful only when it is an activity of service to the world, to all mankind. For this reason, it can never be a camouflaged effort to further the interests of particular Christian citizens, of more or less Christian communities *or even of the Christian churches* as they are instituted in a particular time and place. Christian political action is, as they say in the Netherlands, "*het volk ten baat,*" that is to say, for the good of the (whole) people. Coming out of the integral Christian task of renewal, Christian political action seeks, not as an activity of any instituted church or group of churches, but as a political activity of the Body of Christ, to reform the world in its political aspect, so that there too an acknowledgment may come of the good and holy Law of God and that thus the blessings that follow upon obedience may be showered upon the life of humanity.

It is not a man-centered activity but an effort to administer the world as a service of God Who is sovereign in the world. All idea, therefore, of political lobbies and pressure groups is excluded from a scripturally directed view of the Christian's political task. Christian political action, I must repeat, has nothing whatsoever to do with a seeking of the particular interests of Christian people, of getting what "our people" want. Unless, of course, we understand "the interests of Christian people" in the integral scriptural sense that the interest of Christian people is the interest not that those Christians have as separate persons over against other persons or groups of citizens, but the interest they have together with all creatures of God, viz. that by subjecting themselves everywhere in their lives to the ordinances of God they are saved, *salus* comes to the people and the world (righteousness exalteth a nation).

1.49 Christian Politics a Witness

As both service and administration the Christian political task is a witness. It is not therefore a question of "winning at the polls." How frequently I have heard Christians say, "If you cannot win at the polls, there is no use in beginning a political action." Dear young friends of the Reformation, we do not enter upon Christian political action because we see a chance of winning. Christian political work is an integral aspect of our Christian life. It has nothing to do with winning. Of course, in any *political* action one is eager to acquire the power to give direction to the life of the State, which, in virtue of its office, has the power of the sword. But, like the rest of the Christian life, political life is first of all a witness. It is a witness to the direction this aspect (too) of our life must take from out of the Word of God if we are to be saved.

In connection with "witness," I think of the words the Rev. Marten Vrieze wrote in his little brochure of a few years ago in the Church and Nation Series entitled *Werker in Een Nieuwe Wereld* (p. 25f.): For witnessing in the scriptural sense "is not just speaking but also doing, subjecting one's own acts to Christ's Word, but also seeking to achieve that obedience to the commandments of Christ, exercising such an influence, that there *comes* in human society a subjection to that Word..."

1.50 Example of A.R.S.S.

I believe that we can use the example of the A.R.S.S. again here. We have drawn up an educational credo. That is our witness. In that creed we express, we confess before God and the world, what we think obedience in higher education involves. But that is not the end of our witness. That is the creed of an organization of people who in common see these things that way. But now the A.R.S.S. is going to go to the people. We all hope and pray – and each of us must do what he can in this next year – that the people will see that there must come a new alignment in this area of Canadian life. That will then be a re-forming of the Canadian people. Then there will come, through their support, a center of Reformed Studies, where a new generation will be educated to go out into the practice of life and work at a more integral re-formation of our life together on this continent. In this way, by gradual steps of obedience, the Kingdom of God insinuates itself, with its peace and joy, into our lives, not because of us or what we do, but because of the re-forming Power of the Word of God in our lives, driving on to a renewal of the problematics. Here we are witnessing in the biblical sense.

The same holds for our political life. We must give positive expression to the central thrust of the Word-revelation of God for our political lives in a "political credo." This is the first step of a witness, to God first and also to the whole world. But we must also seek to achieve an acknowledgment of and subjection to the Norm of God in Canadian political life by bearing down on men with a political action that witnesses properly to the saving Law of a gracious God in Christ and brings a political realignment of human forces.

Before I end, I want to say that the time may come when to engage in such a witness will cost you your head. Indeed, this very day there are Christians whose heads are being cut off, so to speak, and we must pray for them every day, not that they will "win at the polls", but that they may stand in the evil day, and, having done all, to stand. There is a big difference. Who knows when our day will come? We must stand and witness, even when it is painfully obvious that we shall have no influence at the polls. That is the Christian witness in the world, of which our political witness is but an aspect.

In all this political work we are, after all, only humble instruments, by God's grace, of that reconciliation which Christ introduced into our sin-disturbed world, and which continues in the world by means of the operations of the Spirit of Christ in the hearts of those who together make up the Body of Christ.

It is easy to see from what I have said this morning that Christian political thought and action must begin from a point that modern man simply cannot understand. All the things that we have been saying are foolishness in his mind, just plain foolishness. But so, of course, is Christianity itself. There may just possibly be a connection.

Lecture II:
ANTITHESIS

2.1 The Forms of its Political Expression and Their Development in Modern Times

You WILL REMEMBER THAT I am dealing in this conference with the general subject: SCRIPTURAL RELIGION AND POLITICAL TASK.

Yesterday I spoke about a political articulation of the central religious knowledge we have in Jesus Christ. We saw that our whole life, and in particular our political "life," receives its principial direction out of the hold that the Word of God has upon our hearts. We saw in what *sense* the Word of God directs our political "goings" at the beginning. Finally, we took note that a genuinely Christian political life must begin from a point that modern man no longer can understand. It is now my hope that today's lecture will clarify further this last statement.

2.2 Modernity Lives Out of Another Principle

It will probably not come as a surprise to most of you to hear that the political life of the modern world has developed out of (i.e. has been an articulation or elaboration of) a principle quite different from, indeed antithetical to, the scriptural Principle we were talking about yesterday. Its history has been the growing, changing or developing articulation of this antithetical *principle*.

In virtue of the creation-order all our cultural life must articulate or positivize (give a positive form to) a certain religious direction of the heart. The living and powerful Word of God, setting us in the Truth, is the Director, the Arche or Principium of our lives. But there is another something that takes the place of this authentic Principium in the lives of others. The unbeliever *imagines* to himself an authoritative directing principle to take the place of God's *given* authoritative Guide of life, to suppress and to supplant it. This is what the Bible means by the imaginations of the heart of man (cf. Gen. 6:5; Rom. 1:21). Men do not just stand up, look at the facts, and reason about them. The lectures of Prof. Van Riessen at this conference make that very clear. Men do not, as an empiricistic or empirio-criticistic epistemology would have it, just gather in more or less simple sense-data (as "givens" of experience), to order these rationally and thus come to the Truth. Our "experience" does not begin from, is not directed by, such simple psychical *sensa* of our life of sense-perception or an innately possessed logical *a priori*. This is the first and most serious error of current epistemological theories. Man is a *religious* being. He is involved *ab initio* in a radical, central religious "grasping" of the integral sense of things. Primordially in man there is either a religious acceptance of the Truth or a religious distorting suppression of it. Man reacts obediently (having been regenerated and illumined by the Word of God) or disobediently (i.e. suppressingly, distortingly) to the revelatory Light of the Law-order of God (the Order of Creation): he does this in his sense-life, in the forming of his logical concepts, – in short, in all the manners (modes) of his life-expression. In everything he does and thinks he betrays that he is a *religious* being. This is what we mean when we speak of "heart" in the scriptural sense. All of the "issues" of a man's life are from out of his heart.

2.3 Apostate Imagination Suppresses and Distorts

The imagination of the unbeliever's heart is a suppressing something. The unbeliever does not "hear" the Word of God. He suppresses it, because he pushes it down from the place it has in virtue of God's creation-ordinance. That is to say, the unbeliever does this in the *imagination of his heart.* And there too (since there must be religious direction) he substitutes something else for the Word of God. This at once brings a distortion of the Truth at the very center of the unbeliever's life. The unbeliever is a rebel against the Truth. He will not live any longer *anywhere* by the Light of the Truth of God, which is the Health (*Salus*) of the nations.

The rebel cannot *really* change the world. It is anchored in the creation-ordinance, the Will of the sovereign God. God maintains His Thesis. Not being able to make a world in which the relations are other than they really are, rebellious man can only *attempt, in his imagination*, to live in another world that is not real. But even this, of course, can only be an unsuccessful experiment. For there is but one world, and in the world that God made, *he really lives.* The only possibility open to man, the rebel, is to mis-form or distort in his imagination the existing powerful and firmly anchored revelational Truth of God's Thesis. This then is sinful man's anti-thesis, the thesis he would set in the place of God's Thesis. The antithesis cannot have the same status as the Thesis, because the being who "posits" it – even though we carry the line of imagined "positers" back to the Devil himself, the Father of Lies – is *not* the Positer. He can only imagine, in the deceptive imaginings of his darkened heart, that he is a kind of positer, as Kant, for example, imagined man as form-giver for nature, the assigner of meaning, determiner of the constitution of things. The imagined world of the anti-thesis, like all idols, is only an *onding*, something that is really nothing at all. What gives it existence at all is the Thesis, of which the anti-thesis can only be a distortion. Distortion pre-supposes the Original Meaning and Constitution of things, what God made (set down, posited, thetized). As distortion, however, it presents paradoxes, leads to the deterioration and decadence of human life and society and ultimately to the Abyss.

2.4 Proper Use of "Thesis" and "Antithesis"

This way of viewing the matter will be of decisive importance for the way we use the terms "thesis" and "antithesis." Many of you here will recall that in our first Unionville Conference two years ago I uttered a brief word of caution about our use of these two terms. Many Christians speak of themselves somewhat loosely, I am afraid, as the people of the Antithesis. When we say that we are the people of the Antithesis we mean that through the Gospel we understand that there is an *irreconcilable* war, constantly pressing on, dynamically developing towards the end-time (eschaton), a fundamentally antithetical relation between the obedient and the disobedient (rebellious, revolutionary) response of the human heart to the revealed Will of our Sovereign, between those, the prevailing bias of whose lives is one directed by the living and powerful Word of God, and those whose life is a constant effort to suppress the Truth of the Creation-Light (of which the Gospel is a re-publication) and to substitute for it what K. J. Popma once called *antevangelia* or pseudo-gospels, pseudo-light.

2.5 Wrong Use

This is indeed a proper scriptural usage of the term "anti-thesis." Many of us, however – and the swift tempo and pressures of our lives are contributing factors here –, holding fast to the expression "We are the people of the Antithesis," fall without thinking into a second meaning, viz. that the side of this fundamental world-struggle-of-spirits on which the Christian is found is the side of the antithesis. Here "antithesis" no longer refers to the fact of the dividedness of our race but to one of the two sides. The idea then is that the world lies in sin, and now Christians, redeemed by Christ and empowered by His Spirit, come to that world with an *anti*dote.

This manner of describing the situation, as though we come with an opposing principle to a world which has already posited its principle, we being thus the proclaimers of the Antithesis to the world of the supposed Thesis, does not do justice to the central scriptural revelation about the Truth of God. When you say that the Gospel is the position of the Antithesis, you thereby say that there is first a Thesis, over against which the Gospel comes to stand. To say this is to fail to see that the work of Christ restores us to the Truth, that the Gospel is a re-publication of an Order, a Natural Light, that is as old as the creation. As we have frequently said here at Unionville, in Christ we are once more made to "see" the nature of God's world and of our place in it, thus "seeing" also what we have to do. Re-creation points back to the creation. We are brought back to the creation-situation of service within the Law-order of God, which is not "fixed in immutable Being" but is *sure* in Him Who is the Faithful One. As abiding Law-structure it is the Condition or ontic *a priori* of all that happens. God's Word in Christ is a reiteration of what God said when in His deed-revelation He created the world. The Christian who has been saved out of the world has truly had administered to him an antidote to the blindness of that world, but he has, further, been brought back to his creaturely situation of Office-bearing. The Christian position is not the Antithesis but the Thesis (now republished in Christ). The revolt of man, deceived by Satan to think of himself as the Positer of the Truth, against the Thesis of God, – this revolt is the antithetical religious position. The rebel is in opposition to the Truth.

Any movement in the Christian Church which forgets that re-creation brings us back to the creation, and which preaches only that we must be saved out of the world by Christ, even though they may add "saved to serve" (by which they do *not* mean to live according to God's Law in the entire creation, dynamically bringing to positive form all that God has laid potentially in it, driven thereto by the POWER of the Word of God, but simply have in mind "to go out into the world to witness to Christ's saving of the soul and to bring others to Christ"), — any such movement is not sufficiently scripturally directed. It may be pietistical, but we had better speak very clearly of it as an incipient heresy, a first falling away from the integral sense of the divine Word-revelation which directs our life-"goings" from out of the heart.

2.6 Summary of Our View

To keep the world-historical record straight, then, we must be clear on the point that the Truth we have in Christ is God's Truth or Thesis, which not only comes *before* the antithesis of rebellious (revolutionary) man, but also, because of the difference in status between God as the real Positer and the creature as only an imagined Positer, is *presupposed* in all apostate anti-thetical efforts at stating and living the Truth. The Lie depends upon the Truth for its formulation. Statements of the antithesis can only be understood in the light of the Thesis. Life that proceeds from an antithetical religious principle can only be grasped when seen in the light of the Truth. We need the light of the Word of God to understand properly what apostate man is doing.

2.7 Importance for Understanding Historical Movements

It is extremely important to bear all these things in mind when we undertake, as we are doing on this second morning of our conference, to understand historical movements. Speaking generally, only within the last century have men set themselves seriously and systematically to thinking about what is involved in the making of historical judgments. How do we understand the meaning of historical events? Of course, we cannot go into this question now, but we can say this, that if our understanding of such events arises from within the stream of historical development itself, we are condemned to a position we "sense" in our bones cannot be true, viz. historical relativism. This would mean, for instance, that a mid-nineteenth century German Junker could see in the Protestant Reformation only that which *his* own historical situatedness permitted him to see, and that a mid-twentieth century American business-minded investigator would only be able to see in the same movement that which *his* (historically conditioned) life allowed him to see. Each picture of the Protestant Reformation would be different, individually acquired, having no general validity. On this view we see an historical event *relative* to the place in the historical flow that we ourselves occupy. This is *historical relativism*. Men have been and still are deeply concerned about this problem. (A very important book in this historic discussion is Ernst Troeltsch, *Der Historismus und seine Probleme*. In English you can read, for example, Maurice Mandelbaum, *The Problem of Historical Knowledge*.) For if it be true, then in the history of historical judgments (say, about the Protestant Reformation) we have to do, not with an approach to the *true meaning* of that movement, but only with a succession of personal, historically relative judgments, and there is no Criterion, itself *not* limited to an historical time and place, that enables us to judge *the truth of the Protestant Reformation*.

2.8 Vain Attempts to Escape Historical Relativism

It will not do, as a way out of the difficulty, to say that the twentieth century investigator of the Protestant Reformation must pull down the shades, so to speak, upon the twentieth century round about him and lose himself in the records of the sixteenth. For the twentieth century is not merely all about us, it is *in* us. *We* are, in a very real sense, the twentieth century. It will not do, either, for a classical scholar to say that he has an absolutely convincing feeling that the fourth century before Christ was the greatest and most important century in history; for we can bring forward a Henry Adams who had the same feeling about the twelfth century of the Christian era. It can easily be argued that each comes to his judgment about history out of his own situatedness in history.

Undoubtedly, we men are deeply influenced by our position in history, and it is a gain to have been made vividly aware of it. But the man who makes historical judgments is, in the deepest level of his existence, not an historical being but a religious being; he stands either in the abiding Truth of God's Word-revelation, thus in Christ made able to "see" something of the real nature of things (and, specifically, of the nature of the Protestant Reformation), or he is fallen away into an imagined anti-thetical substitute which distorts. The Light of the Thesis is necessary to "understanding."

2.9 Religion Involved in Historical Knowledge

An example will, I think, bring out more clearly what I have in mind. If we are to make an historical judgment about the work of the Greek philosopher, Plato, and about his historical connections with other Greek philosophers who preceded and followed him, we must understand what Plato is *really saying*. According to historical relativism we have in the history of historical writing about Plato only a succession of statements about what *later men saw in Plato.* But where is Plato himself? What was actually happening back there in that important development of human life in the fourth century before the Christian era? Is genuine historical knowledge about it *available* to us? And now, further, I would ask, *Can the historian really understand the meaning of what was actually going on* when Plato decided that in addition to this world of constant change there must also be a world of immutable, purely intelligible law-essences, called (to speak of only one kind) "ideas," when he thereby confused law (what it is to be horse) and absolute thing (the horse itself), law and exemplar, or when in meso-platonism and neo-platonism these "ideas" of Plato were turned into an *a priori* thought content of the macrocosmic and microcosmic minds *unless, illumined by the Re-statement of the nature of things in the Gospel of Jesus Christ, he has sensed the place and role of the Law in the cosmos?* Law is not "a thing apart," nor is it an exemplar. [One cannot – to relate this to a matter we were discussing yesterday – look upon Christ in His historical appearance as the Exemplar (Law) and ask oneself, What would Jesus do?, as if that were the Law for our life, but must look to the Law of God, to which Christ the man was also subject.] But having been enlightened by the Thesis (in its re-publication, of course), the Christian historian is in a position not only to "see": 1) what it is in the creation-structure that Plato in his analysis is occupied with, what in the nature of things his thought *refers to*; at the same time he is made aware of: 2) the (religious) *distortion* in Plato's anti-thetical statement about the Law.

The same situation prevails when we set ourselves to making historical judgments about the development of the political life of western man. It is impossible to appraise the history properly, to "understand," to know the real nature of the several "parties" or "camps" or "minds" or "movements" of our western political wrestling-of-spirits unless we are aware of the central and integral sense of the Word of God. A knowledge of the Thesis is always prerequisite to an understanding of the various historically worked out statements of the antithesis made by men who are fallen away from the Truth.

But it is also true – exactly as in the case of the historian's "understanding" Plato – that we must not only "see" the political grouping, alignments, constellations, movements of our time in the light of the divine Thesis, but also, in its light, *see these movements.* In our Office in Christ we must listen *painfully and carefully* to what is being said and done. No amount of religious understanding will enable us to judge the spirit of Plato *if we do not seriously listen to Plato.* We are called to discern the spirits, and that involves long and laborious study, away from the pressures and plaudits of men. We have to "experience" the political life of the modern world for what it is. What most modern scholars overlook is that both the investigator and the human actions being investigated are in their roots religious. Only when we attempt to understand historical movements in this way are we prophetic as God in His creation made us to be. Only thus do we really address ourselves to our contemporaries and to our time in the Name of Christ, as His servants, beseeching them (and it) to be reconciled unto God.

2.10 Malaise of Political World

In this spirit we now turn to survey – very briefly, of course – the modern political "world." When we overlook such "immediacies" of contemporary political life as the Berlin Crisis and attempt to "see" the nature of the political "world" of our time, we are struck by one thing in particular: the political MALAISE. Nowhere do we find those great MEN of God which the Word thoroughly furnishes unto every good work, who see their political task in the way we spoke of it yesterday. No statesmen working to restore human society in its political aspect to a healthy body. No big principle operative in political action. No corporative unity of political leaders and people. Instead, MALAISE. Little politicians dealing with one immediate (supposedly technical) problem after another. Little people, scurrying from one pressing political distress point to another as the disaster sirens scream, i.e. as political events force them; hopping blindly, like rabbits, at the crack of a gunshot. The vigorous pursuit of political life is a rare thing in the West. Everywhere we observe lassitude and ebbing life. And the split between a political elite and the uninterested masses.

For example, we all know how hard it is to get people out to vote, even (in the U.S.A.) for the governor of a state. Those who attempt to remedy this immediate situation do it in the spirit of the time, i.e. they try to find a way, by means of a type of propaganda that is deemed suitable, to attract the voter's interest. Put on TV a (so-called) beautiful woman displaying the newest eyelid shading as one who will vote for your candidate. Find a candidate for political office who is photogenic, a ladies' man, a man's man, etc.

Of course, there are men who find in the "game of politics" as it is played at present a road to personal positions of power and influence, to a fuller social existence. Locally, young Republicans or Democrats may be expected to bring up enough enthusiasm to organize a "binge" of a parade the night before an election. The fun's the thing. And besides, there is always the possibility of a larger sphere of personal acquaintance and influence, perhaps of financial opportunity and power. But these things must not be mistaken for signs of genuine political life. All these busy-nesses are a concern with *unrelated* things, in order to disguise the nothing-ness behind all the busy-ness.

There is truth in the observation that very many people are so busy securing their material prosperity (i.e. amassing things and money) that they have no time left for a genuine interest in political life. *Fortune* magazine, for instance, in March, 1955 announced as its conclusion from a poll it had taken that typical young business-men of 25 years of age liked the "middle-road philosophy [of Eisenhower Republicanism — H.E.R.]... not so much for its actual content as for the fact that it provides a logical cover for the absence of political opinion." Here we see the incipient nihilism of an influential segment of our younger generation. By declaring for a middle-road position they were giving every appearance of participating – as all good citizens should! – in the political life of their country without, however, involving themselves in the responsibility of having committed themselves clearly to a definite choice of political direction, and all that while yet leaving themselves free to pursue their business careers without interference. These young men hoped that the "progressive moderation" would keep things as they were without any crises, so that they could go on accumulating wealth. (An interesting aspect of our present effete "conservatism.")

2.11 An Aspect of the General Cultural Apathy

This lack of genuine interest in the direction of political life is but an aspect of our life in general. While I was writing these lectures, an article appeared drawing attention to the exorbitantly high crime rate in our national capital. The indignant writer has this to say:

The American people might be expected to be alarmed and ashamed of the condition represented by these statistics. There is no evidence of alarm, shame or, even, interest. This writer… believes the general citizenry is uninterested because it does not give a hoot about the capital city of the United States. The citizens like to vacation here, visit the White House, look at Congress. That is all. Mere curiosity.

A couple of years ago, a well-known American financier and writer on international affairs, in a speech before the American Academy of Political and Social Science declared that the overall postwar foreign policy of the United States has not been successful because of the "ignorance, indifference and self-satisfaction" of the American people. "The most obvious cause contributing to our nation's failure as a world leader," he stated, "is ignorance – ignorance of geography, ignorance of languages and cultures other than our own and, above all, ignorance of history." "We are ignorant," he went on, "not because knowledge is beyond our reach, but because we are not interested enough to reach for it. Our ignorance is an expression of a curious indifference." "We live", he said, "as if nothing much mattered except new cars, new houses, new clothes, new gadgets and lower taxes."

The man who spoke those words concluded, however, by saying that our indifference may stem from the fact that the average American "has become more and more alienated from the democratic processes of decision-making." He further sees the cause of this alienation in the fact that the decision-making has increasingly been taken over by "big business and big government." In this last I cannot agree with him. First "big business" and "big government" *had to develop*. First there had to be in society the possibility for these two "bigs" to take over. No; the cause of the disease lies deeper. *Everywhere* we look, even in the lives of individuals, we find the same political MALAISE. Whatever we may think in detail about western political life, in general it displays more the features of political death than of political life. (An apparent exception is to be seen in the emergence of the socialist and communist movements. We shall discuss this phenomenon at the proper place.)

2.12 No Meaningful Choice

Nevertheless, a closer look will, I am sure, reveal that it is not just a whoring after material possessions that explains the lack of a genuine political *life* in the West. On the contrary, a very good case, I believe, could be made for the proposition that the concentration upon securing material prosperity would not have developed to the degree it has if at an earlier stage a genuinely Christian effort had been made in political life to *provide a really meaningful choice of political directions*. Where men see no meaning, can find no way out, they turn to the securing of their personal lives and, in extremis, that seems often to come down to amassing economic wealth. Think of the Jews who escaped from Hitler's Fortress Europe. Think of the mercenary generation that appeared in Athens at the end of the Peloponnesian Wars, when Greek political life was in a state of collapse. That something of this sort is involved seems to me to be clear.

Even the politicians who run for office appear to have difficulty in finding real issues of any magnitude on which to compete with their contestants. More and more, political life appears to our contemporaries as a technical matter. If the office-holders are only "good" people – and that means people, for example, who have no compromising contacts with the "underworld," the "booze" industry, white slave traffic, etc. – and are "competent," the solution of the problems will undoubtedly come in due course, *regardless of party affiliation*, professed platforms, etc. More and more we get Citizens Actions for "good" government, non-party politics on the local level (where the problems are "technical"), and such like. I told you yesterday of the Dutch government minister who really seemed to believe that you could hand over all questions of religious world-view to the churches and then have left for the political parties only the technical (!) matters of government. He had apparently even deceived himself into thinking that this solution he was proposing was itself a technical matter!

In my first lecture last year I told you that a Cornell University sociologist recently reported that American college students are "politically disinterested [she undoubtedly means "uninterested" – H.E.R.] and apathetic." But it is true that everywhere the eye falls on western political life it marks a state of APATHY, aimless drifting, meaninglessness, nihilism. The explanation this sociologist gave of the apathy of the college students is, I believe, significant. They are (politically) apathetic, she said, because "there are no clearly defined programs around which to rally, no clearly defined answers to the problems their generation confronts." Another question, of course, is whether the absence of programs and answers is what produces the political malaise, or whether it is itself an expression of the malaise.

The complaint of the students is only the political side of the more general complaint of Bertrand Russell, to which I also referred last year. Russell speaks for a great many of our contemporaries when he says that men cannot discover a single clear aim to be striven after or a single clear principle that could lead them.

In the political area we are brought a big step closer to the real situation when we read in Stanley Knowles' book *The New Party* (p. 4) that along with political disillusionment and apathy, in Canadian politics has come "the clear recognition of its basic cause, the lack of any real line of demarcation between the two old parties." Here the lack of political vitality is specifically ascribed to the Tweedledum-Tweedledee character of the liberal-conservative "polarity."

2.13 Liberal-Conservative

What is meant by the liberal-conservative polarity? What is meant by its Tweedledum-Tweedledee character? How does the character here ascribed to it "cause" political apathy? With respect to the third of these questions Knowles replies somewhat like this: a parliamentary system functions properly only if the political parties operating within it – and they are essential to its proper functioning – represent real differences that offer clear-cut alternatives, thus providing society with the opportunity to make real choices; but recent Canadian history has brought many people to the realization that there are no real differences between the two old parties, that the present constellation of political life in Canada accordingly offers them no significant choice of political directions, and that it therefore makes little difference whether one votes Liberal or Conservative, or indeed whether one votes at all, except perhaps to cast a (cynical?) protest vote for a minor party which can rally but little political power in Canada.

To ask the above questions brings us to the very heart of our subject for this second lecture, and although it will take a little time to formulate answers to them, the answers will, I am certain, bring with them a surprising amount of insight into the present sickly condition of the western political world and what task is laid upon us Christians in this situation in the light of the divine Thesis.

We can say without much fear of contradiction that the political life of the modern western world has largely revolved around the two poles of liberalism (or progressivism) and conservatism. The very universality of the phenomenon indicates something of the central place it must have in any explanation of western political life.

2.14 Holds Also for America

Upon first thought, some might be inclined to deny that the tags "liberal" and "conservative" can be used to account in any sound or significant way for the political life of the United States. Certainly, it cannot be said that, of the two major political parties in the U.S.A., the Democratic party represents the movement of liberalism and the Republican party that of conservatism. On the contrary, such is definitely not the case. We are all quite familiar with the fact that the big American political parties are not in the first place rallying points of political conviction at all, but only more or less opportunistic associations of various economic, social and political interests, – marriages, one might call them, of utility. It is an aspect of the crisis in our political life in the U.S.A. that our parties are so hopelessly divided in their political point of view. For the fact remains, as Groen van Prinsterer and Napoleon, among others, so well knew, that the real powers in life, the mainsprings and directors of cultural life and development, are convictions of faith. (Was it not Napoleon himself who said that in calculating the forces at one's disposal for waging war, morale was to numbers as three to one?) If the American parties wish to become significant as directors of political life, they will have to embrace clear-cut *political* points of view, a *political* creed. That they do not now have this character is one more piece of evidence that political life has undergone deterioration, that it has become the means of insuring that certain chiefly economic groups are maintained in positions of power, that it lends itself for the communist war of the (economic) classes. Political life has been metamorphosed into a function of economic life. But then it does not function in the *political* way. It has lost its *political structure and meaning*. Meanwhile, though the two parties themselves may not represent the two modern political attitudes of conservatism and liberalism (progressivism), *our real political groupings* do. The fact is simply that in the U.S.A. the genuine political groupings, which often lead to the actual voting blocks, cannot be identified with the party-organizations. These latter do not represent whatever there is in the U.S.A. of genuine *political* belief. Our political life remains of the progressivist or conservativist stamp. The parties are *politically* largely meaningless.

A book recently published in the U.S.A. contains this bit of dialogue relevant to the point we are here making. A man in one of the government departments in Washington, D.C. is talking to a military man just returned from overseas service. The government man says, "Let's see, now, you've been away for about two years. Can you still name the two major political groupings in the United States?" Somewhat puzzled, the returned military man replies, "Why, the Democrats and the Republicans, I suppose. Don't they far outnumber all others?" To which the government man responds, "Not anymore, Junior. Those are only 'fronts' for voting purposes. There's a different lineup today, which crosses all regular party lines. Today most Americans can be classified into two major political groups – the Liberals and the Conservatives. There are Liberal Republicans and Conservative Democrats, for example. And, just to confuse you, today neither word means what it used to mean."

I quote this not because of any particular merit the book may have, but simply because it sums up a fact or two observed by many. The real political life of the U.S.A. is divided into the two classifications of liberalism and conservatism, just as everywhere else in the western world. And the terms do not always refer, or, at least, seem to refer, to the same thing.

At present the precise significance of this universal phenomenon of western political life is the subject of a very live debate. Much reflection is being given to it. A look into our magazines dealing with historical, political and ethical subjects will disclose that in the past decade many excellent articles have been devoted to it. The books on the subject of conservatism and liberalism are even better known. A revival, of a sort, of some kind of conservatism in America after the Second World War has brought the whole problem of this political polarity into prominent discussion and made it a timely topic.

2.15 Meaning of Conservative and Liberal

A first difficulty is the determination of the meaning of the terms "conservatism" and "liberalism." On this point we find a great deal of confusion in the magazine articles. Take, for instance, the term "conservatism." Naturally, the meaning of this term has something to do with conserving or preserving. It looks to the past. It has in view keeping in good condition what already exists, what has been handed down to us in the tradition. But confusion arises as soon as one asks about *what* it is that is to be conserved. For example, the positions of many people who call themselves conservatives in 1961 would have been considered quite liberal in the 1920's. The question therefore is, what point and state of affairs in history does one take as that which ought to be conserved? Or does the conservative simply follow along after more radical spirits, busying himself with conserving what those more radical spirits have championed and fought to achieve? If this is the case, can conservatism be a very significant position in its own right? What then can it possibly oppose in the progressivism of the more progressive spirits if in a few years its task will be to conserve progressivism's conquests? Does conservatism simply look with a skeptical, or perhaps even jaundiced, eye at all *innovation* as such? Hence, the complaint of some writers on the subject that the tag "conservatism" has been used to justify any existing order, at any stage of history; that one does not find in conservative circles any indication of the character of the political institutions and way of life conservatism as an ideology would be interested in defending. The charge that is brought against conservatism as an ideology is that it "lacks what might be termed a substantive ideal." If this is the case, we can understand the recent newspaper report that in Khrushchev's Russia the charge of "conservatism" has been levelled against old Comrade Molotov! But we must ponder more seriously the argument of a recent writer that the *conservative* movement in America has been the conserving of the *liberal* tradition, that both major political parties follow liberal traditions and therefore – inasmuch as the American Revolution was deeply influenced by the ideas of the Enlightenment and these ideas probably still represent the strongest moral and intellectual force sustaining American culture – in this specific American sense are *conservative*.

With the terms "liberalism" and "progressivism" the situation is not always a great deal clearer. What is meant by being progressive? Progress to *what*? Why would conservatives have to be opposed to this progress? In fact, do not conservatives frequently express their desire for real progress? The fact is that liberalism, just as much as conservatism, seems to lack a "substantive ideal." Both "progressive" and "conservative" become meaningless apart from their relation to a belief about *what ought to be done*, apart from their relation to a Norm. They then appear to glide into each other's territory. A joke in last night's newspaper described "the man at the next desk" as "a radical middle-of-the-roader." Richard Hofstadter tells us in his book *The American Political Tradition* that Woodrow Wilson, in proposing that the State's power be used to *restore* pristine American ideals, spoke these words: "If I did not believe that to be progressive was to preserve the essentials of our institutions, I for one could not be a progressive." Interesting words to ponder, indeed. Would not all genuine progress preserve a certain continuity with the accumulation of past wisdom as embodied in our institutions? But is this now conservative progressivism or progressive conservativism? No; I am not joking. Hofstadter describes Wilson's conversion from conservatism to progressivism as something "no more drastic than a change of emphasis." More generally, he would argue in the book I mentioned that our American politicians, liberal and conservative, have had more in common with each other than the agitated rhetoric of political controversy usually suggests.

Is it possible that there is a general drift to "liberal" positions, and that the conservative comes, bit by slow bit, along the *same road*? This very *gliding* feature then would make conservatism largely meaningless as a *director* of political life or as a *dynamic alternative* in political life to liberalism. Liberalism would seem to be in that case the dynamic leader-out-in-front, and the conservative the one who is steadily adapting to it, adopting its positions.

Indeed, the above analysis would seem to fit much that we have known as conservatism in Canada and the U.S.A. It would explain the fact that today's conservatives represent yesterday's liberalism, that the "safe" position would be a conservative progressivism or a progressive conservatism, or middle-road "Eisenhower Republicanism." Such a "middle" would then represent the general drift. Proponents of such a position would be assured of riding "the wave of the future" without sticking their necks out too far to be calumniated as "reformers" (in the sense, then, of "revolutionaries"). At the same time, it would be a confession that modern political life, as represented by these two "movements," is travelling but *one road*; that, accordingly, *a genuine choice of directions* is not provided in this type of structure of political life because there is no difference of direction between conservatism and progressivism but only a difference in tempo along the one (inevitable?) path of progress marked by our increasing rational-technical (!) mastery of the conditions of our existence. In that case, however, we are not so very far removed from the judgment made by Stanley Knowles that the cause of the present political apathy is the Tweedledum-Tweedledee character of the liberal-conservative polarity.

2.16 Thetical Interruption

Having come to this point where we can begin to see the sense of asserting the basic similarity of conservatism and liberalism – at least in North America; for it has been argued that British and continental conservatism involves more of an opposition to the fundamental ideas of the French Revolution, that have (supposedly) inspired the liberalistic tradition –, I interrupt our discussion of the meaning of the development of the forms of modern political life for just a moment in order to make a *thetical* statement. Conservation and progress are two features that *together* should mark all human cultural work. When God placed man in Office, He described his Task in these words: to dress and keep the garden. Man was to "keep" what was already present as a "good," and he was to "dress," i.e. dynamically to bring about an as yet non-existent situation that preserved what was good from out of the past but also further developed it to the greater glory of God. Both this "keeping" and this "dressing," however, can be understood properly only in connection with the divine Thesis or Law-order of the creation.

A consideration of this scriptural revelation will make clear why conservatism and liberalism or progressivism cannot offer a genuine choice of directions in political life. To be sure, conservatism is not the same as conserving or "keeping," and progressivism is not the same as "dressing" or development. Both "ism" words, as I have suggested to you in each of the previous conferences, suggest a falling away from the original integral insight and a raising of an aspect or partial insight to the place of an absolute. Conservatism can then easily turn into anti-progressive reaction, and progressivism can just as easily become a blind zeal for something "new," whether that "new" is genuine progress or not. (To know whether development is progress requires knowledge of a Norm.) But true conservation and true progress always belong *together*: genuine conservation involves belief in God's faithful maintaining of His Law (on the basis of which dynamic development can take place; for a scriptural view of Law is not identical with static theories about "natural law"), and genuine progress means working in the way of *past* fruitful obedience to the divine Law towards the expanding future Consummation of Christ's Kingdom of Righteousness.

Genuine conservation and genuine progress must together characterize all human cultural activity; they cannot then be made to be a choice of opposing directions of life. Yet there is in life a two-ness of direction which requires *radical choice*. As we have seen, the two *religious* ways of men will also come to expression, unless the real nature of things is obscured, in political life. This real difference in the direction of our ways can, however, never be expressed, for the reason given, in terms of conservatism and progressivism. How then? That is the problem.

2.17 Religious Fixing of Meaning

Before I can give an answer to that question, I must say something more about modern political conservatism and progressivism. Already we have observed that apart from a reference to some 'norm' these movements are deprived of substantial meaning. Much of the confusion to be found in discussions of them is to be ascribed to the too narrow limits within which they are frequently considered; for this political polarity is a universal feature of modern western political life that had its origin in that fertile focal point of modern history that we know as the French Revolution. From that point in history it has spread out over the entire western world (and much farther). We can grasp the real meaning of "conservatism" and "progressivism," and of the political structure of polarity that these two movements are thought of as constituting, only when we investigate them *at the point of their historical emergence*. That moment in history provides a point of orientation – even, as we shall see, a kind of norm – by which to "see" (religiously) the meaning of these phenomena (discern their "spirits").

2.18 The French Revolution

What, then, was the French Revolution? In all the writing of the last century and a half the constellation of events that goes by this name stands out above everything else. From the first, men everywhere were somehow fascinated by it. Almost without exception English men of letters greeted the revolutionary movement in France as the dawn of a new day of hope for all mankind. You recall how Wordsworth, reflecting later upon those first days of the Revolution, penned the oft quoted lines:

Bliss was it in that dawn to be alive,
But to be young was very Heaven.

Burke, on the other hand, abhorred what he saw. But all men, however they viewed it, had a kind of presentiment that they "had to do with" what was taking place there in France. Ever since, men have unceasingly been attempting to determine their positions with respect to the awesome event. The idea that the French Revolution was a world revolution fundamentally affecting all humanity dates from the eighteenth century itself. In 1796 Edmund Burke wrote: "It is not France extending a foreign empire over other nations; it is a sect aiming at universal empire, and beginning with the conquest of France."

In our own time there has been a strong return to the view that the French Revolution is perhaps the most fundamental event of modern times. Karl Jaspers, the German existentialist philosopher, writes of it that "it was an event without precedent in human history, and that since the French Revolution there is a specifically new awareness of the epoch-making significance of the time." In 1955 there was published in Germany a book which has as its theme the plastic arts of the nineteenth and twentieth centuries as symptom and symbol of the times. The author, Hans Sedlmayer, art historian at Munchen, believes that art history does not belong to itself alone, but serves to give us a knowledge of man. Listen to the opening words of his book *Verlust der Mitte* (my own translation):

In the years and decades before 1789 an inner revolution set in in Europe, the range of which the mind could not discern: the events we group together under the name "French Revolution" are themselves only a more visible aspect of this awful inner catastrophe. Up to the present we have not succeeded in getting a firm hold on the situation this event has created, neither in the spiritual nor in the practical realm. To understand what there took place is perhaps the most vital task assigned the historical sciences in general: in this turning-point of history we are interested not only as *historians*, but quite immediately as *men*. For with it our present begins, and from it we come to know our situation, come to know ourselves.

That last is certainly the case with our understanding of our political situation. But what is it that makes the Revolution so fundamental, that lends it the power so to fascinate men everywhere ever since it took place?

2.19 Recent Interpretation of the Revolution

Edmund Burke had already used *religious* language to describe the Revolution when he spoke of it as a sect aiming at universal empire. He warned the men of his time that this was not just a change of dynasty such as history has repeatedly given us to see, but *a new kind of political event*. It was, to be sure, a reaction against the traditional world, but it went much deeper than that. It was nothing less than a revolt of men against an order that they had not themselves put there, a revolt against the divine Order of Creation.

After Burke a reaction set in against this interpretation of the Revolution, and many men have attempted to see it as an effort to solve a peculiarly French, though unusually deep, social-economic crisis. (The age of positivism!) But in the most recent decades a remarkable change of opinion is to be observed. Again historians are returning to the view that the most important thing about the French Revolution was its fundamental ideology. The Revolution is again being described as a breaking out in a violent manner into the public life of the revolutionary ideas of modern man. Some even venture to speak of those revolutionary ideas as a living faith. Even Burke's idea that it was a *world*-revolution has been rehabilitated. For instance, Prof. Georges Lefebre of the Sorbonne, whose *The Coming of the French Revolution* was published in 1930 and translated into English in 1947 by Prof. R.R. Palmer, Dodge Prof. of History at Princeton University, re-wrote his book in 1951, completely recasting it to show the supra-national implications of the Revolution. The idea gains ground that the revolutions in Switzerland, those of 1830, 1848, etc., the South American revolutions, the Russian revolution and much of the revolutionary spirit of Asia and Africa belongs to *one continuing movement* of the human spirit. The period of history since the French Revolution has been called the Age of Revolution, and men speak of "a permanent revolution."

A religious war, so had Edmund Burke characterized the French Revolution. Groen van Prinsterer too saw the *religious nature* of these events, and described their deeper intention as "*een omkering der goddelijke orde*," i.e. an overturning of the divine Order. We shall come a great step farther when we understand in what sense this phrase rightly describes the Revolution.

2.20 The Revolution and Rationalism

Discussions of the underlying meaning of the Revolution often relate it to the movement of the human spirit in the eighteenth century that we speak of as the Enlightenment, or the Age of Reason. To this I have no objection, provided that we also see this eighteenth century Enlightenment as a second stage in the continuing development of the new spirit of *rationalism*, the revolutionary movement of thought that arose in the seventeenth century and dominated both it and the following two centuries. This rationalistic spirit signified modern man's radical break with the Christian religion. Of the Age of Reason Charles Frankel once wrote: "In the view of historians, the general pattern of the Age of Reason can be identified. Its unity of purpose had a decisive effect on the course of subsequent historical development." And then:

> The special effort of the Enlightenment was to find a foundation in every field, from the profane sciences to revelation, from music to morals, and theology to commerce, such that thinking and action could be made independent of speculative metaphysics and super-natural revelation. Religion was treated mainly as an appendage to morals and discussed as though it were a part of physics. History was written to place European life in balanced perspective among other ways of life, none of which enjoyed the special sanction of God. In politics, the conception of divine right and supernatural providence were replaced by "the social contract", so that governments could be evaluated as instruments of human desire. In moral philosophy the effort was to base moral codes on Natural Law or on the "well-established facts" of human psychology...

It is important to notice what is here said about politics. Although the statement is oriented more to eighteenth century Enlightenment, the fact is that the eighteenth century did not

really develop a new political theory; it called for political action on the basis of the rationalistic theory of the seventeenth
century. Rousseau is the key figure here. For he is regarded as
the one who gave to the French Revolution its definitive character, i.e. its tendency to *abstract* organization, and, to look
ahead for a moment, he is the writer *par excellence* of liberalism.
Yet the ideas of his *Contrat Social* and other political writings
are largely to be found in Locke and Grotius and Pufendorf.
These ideas belong to the modern rationalist movement generally. Their revolutionary character, even already in the *De jure
belli et pacis* of Hugo Grotius (1625), is to be seen in the hope
he cherishes for an international amity based on a Law of Nature. "War, violence, disorder, which the law of God does not
repress but suffers rather, and even justifies, as being part of an
inscrutable design, all the ills which man is heir to – perhaps
the day will come when some human law will bring about their
mitigation, their abolition. Thus" – I am quoting the famous
French historian, Paul Hazard – "we are invited, with manifold
excuses for such boldness, to pass from the Order of Providence
to the Order of Humanity." Instead of an Order of God, an
order of man. Instead of the Law of God, the social contract.
Instead of the sovereignty of God, the sovereignty of the people
(popular sovereignty, *volkssouvereiniteit*, majority vote, etc.).

2.21 The Spirit of the Age

Since Christians in America often argue that the French Revolution was related to continental thought, more radical than
our Anglo-Saxon background, and that therefore such analyses
as we are here engaged in are really irrelevant to an understanding of North American cultural life, it may be well to call at-

tention to the name of Locke in the above account. Locke and the English Deists had a great influence upon Voltaire, who revivified these ideas upon his return to France. One cannot really distinguish English and Continental here. The ideas are common to the modern rationalist movement. We have to do here with the spirit of an age. The ideas are everywhere.

Let me quote Ernst Cassirer on the subject. "The political rationalism of the seventeenth century," he tells us,

> was a rejuvenation of Stoic ideas. This process began in Italy, but after a short time it spread over the whole of European culture. In rapid progress Neo-Stoicism passed from Italy to France; from France to the Netherlands; to England, to the American colonies... When Thomas Jefferson, in 1776, was asked by his friends to prepare a draft of the American Declaration of Independence he began it by the famous words: "We hold these truths to be self-evident, that all men are created equal; that they are endowed by their Creator with certain unalienable rights; that among these are life, liberty, and the pursuit of happiness. That, to secure these rights, governments are instituted among men, deriving their just powers from the consent of the governed." When Jefferson wrote these words, he was scarcely aware that he was speaking the language of Stoic philosophy. This language could be taken for granted; for since the times of Lipsius and Grotius it had a common place with all the great political thinkers. The ideas were regarded as fundamental axioms that were not capable of further analysis and in no need of demonstration. For they expressed the essence of man and the very character of human reason. The American Declaration of Independence had been preceded and prepared by an even greater event: by the intellectual Declaration of Independence that we find in the theoreticians of the seventeenth century. It was here

that reason had first declared its power and its claim to rule the social life of men. It had emancipated itself from the guardianship of theological thought; it could stand its own ground" (*The Myth of the State*, paperback edition, p. 208ff.).

In the same work (p. 221f.) we read:

The writers of the Great Encyclopedia and the fathers of American democracy, men like D'Alembert, Diderot, and Jefferson, would scarcely have understood the question whether their ideas were new. All of them were convinced that these ideas were in a sense as old as the world. They were regarded as something that has been always, everywhere and believed by all: *quod semper, quod ubique, quod ab omnibus* (the ancient formula for Catholic orthodoxy!). "La raison", said La Bruyere, "est de tous les climats."

2.22 Concept of Ratio

We must take a closer look at this concept of Reason, if we wish to understand the revolutionary character of the modern movement of rationalism. Descartes can best be used to illustrate its meaning. This man, often called the father of the "modern" way of philosophizing, found himself in the midst of life, after having enjoyed the best secondary education available in Europe, his mind a curious mixture of truth and falsehood. His (religious!) need for certainty led him after a while to consider the system of geometrical thought of his day as a model of the perfect clarity he desired in all his experience. In the proofs of geometry every step carries its clarity and necessity with it. A particular step in the proof of a theorem follows with the necessity of logical demonstration from the previous step, and each previous step out of the foregoing, until at last we get back to the first axioms and postulates out of which the entire system is generated. What, now, about these beginnings of geometrical thought? They too are clear and necessary. Not in the way of logical (deductive) demonstration, but because they shine by their own rational light. They are self-evidencing. They are absolute Truth. Descartes now proceeded to enlarge this that he finds in geometry to be the structure of all human thought, which is always essentially geometrical thought. All successive steps of reasoning can be proved by logical deduction; the starting-points are certain *innate ideas*, bearing in themselves the Light of Truth. This body of innate ideas – the ideas of Plato made *a priori* concepts in the philosophy of the Hellenistic Age and found clearly in the reasoning of Aurelius Augustinus – Descartes called the ratio or *lumen naturale* (natural light, light of nature if by "nature" one understands our rational nature).

2.23 Concept of Ratio, the Result of Apostate Religion

Here in this *ratio* or Reason we find the key to the religious and revolutionary character of the rationalist movement generally, more specifically now of the Enlightenment and the French Revolution. This ratio is not just our human power of understanding. It is the understanding, directed by supposed *a priori* or innate ideas, considered as the original Light and Truth that shows us how to "go," how to conduct our lives. The *ratio* or Reason of the rationalist is more than mere rational thinking; in this concept rational thought contains within itself the *Principium* of our life which directs all our ways. This concept is the result of apostate religion; it is a repressing substitute for the Word of God, the true *Principium* which leads us into ways of salvation. It is thus an idol, an "*onding*," something that does not exist and can (and then as *a distortion of the Truth*) only be conceived because in the Truth of the divine Thesis there is the Principium of the divine Word. In this modern rationalism – now the meaning of the term will be clearer – men have replaced God's own sovereign and gracious Word of redemption with their own deepest, rational self as the Light, the Law-word, the directing Principle of our entire life.

2.24 Rationalistic Political Theory

This was true not only of the 'world' of physical things, but also of the 'worlds' that aesthetics and ethics deal with, and also with the 'world' of political life. Hobbes always sought a theory of the body politic that would be equal in clarity, in scientific method, and in certainty to the Galilean theory of physical bodies. And Hugo Grotius firmly believes that we can develop a "mathematics of politics." At this point, as Cassirer tells the story, there "arose another question that was of vital importance for the further development of political thought. Granted that it is possible, and even necessary, to demonstrate a political or ethical truth in the same way as a mathematical truth – where can we find the *principle* of such a demonstration? If there is a "Euclidean" method of politics we must assume that, in this field too, we are in possession of certain axioms and postulates that are incontrovertible and infallible. Thus it became the first aim of any political theory to find out and to formulate these axioms" (*The Myth of the State*, paperback, p. 208).

Most of the seventeenth century thinkers felt, however, that these primordial rational principles of man's political life had been found long ago. They had only to be expressed "in logical language, the language of clear and distinct ideas. To find them, one had only to dispel the clouds that hitherto have obscured the clear light of reason – to forget all our preconceived opinions and prejudices." As Reason (*ratio*), our thought is directed by an absolutely sure and clear (self-evidencing) Beginning that directs in a definite way and that is nothing else than an *a priori* root-part of our rational human nature. Every thinking man, when he (rightly) carries his investigation back to the source or root-origin of his thought, will accordingly become aware of the fundamental principles for life. Truth is Everyman's. It is in this connection that Cassirer speaks of Thomas Jefferson and the opening words of the American Declaration of Independence (see them quoted above). Jefferson and the men of his time believed that what they said was nothing other than the "common sense" of the matter, whatever matter it was that was being thought about. The assumptions were that the rational is the real and the real is the rational, that the rational is clear to every (properly) thinking man, and that rational truth is the same in all ages and climes (since Reason is always and everywhere the same).

These thoughts can all be found, at least in seed form, in the work of Rene Descartes, the first paragraph of whose *Discourse on Method* reads as follows:

> Good sense is, of all things among men, the most equally distributed; for everyone thinks himself so abundantly provided with it, that those even who are the most difficult to satisfy in everything else, do not usually desire a larger measure of this quality than they already possess. And in this it is not likely that all are mistaken: the conviction is rather to be held as testifying that the power of

judging aright and of distinguishing Truth from Error, which is properly what is called Good Sense or Reason, is by nature equal in all men; and that the diversity of our opinions, consequently, does not arise from some being endowed with a larger share of Reason than others, but solely from this, that we conduct our thoughts along different ways, and do not fix our attention on the same objects. For to be possessed of a vigorous mind is not enough; its prime requisite is rightly to apply it. The greatest minds, as they are capable of the highest excellencies, are open likewise to the greatest aberrations; and those who travel very slowly may yet make far greater progress, provided they keep always to the straight road, than those who, while they run, forsake it.

2.25 This Political Rationalism the Basis of Modern Democracy

These assumptions of Descartes and of the rationalist movement became the intellectual – actually, *religious* – basis for the social and political institutions of modern democracy. If "the diversity of our opinions" is the result merely of the fact that we do not all find an adequate way of applying our rational powers, then a system of universal, public education is all that is needed to raise all men to the level of enlightened and responsible citizenship. This was the conclusion a subsequent century drew. Then we could put our confidence in the popular will and the popular vote, and acquiesce in the will of the majority.

This rationalistic basis of our modern democracies is one form – a subjectivistic one – of *the theory of natural law* (where "natural" refers to our rational nature, which is the Law). Besides being, as was thought, self-evidencing, this theory could appeal to an unbroken history from the time of Hellenistic (to an important degree Stoic) philosophy, through the Roman jurists, the Church Fathers, the scholastic philosophers and the conciliarists of the late medieval church. This long and unbroken history, in turn, convinced men the more of the self-evidencing character of the rationalist theory. It is to this long history that Walter Lippmann refers when he speaks of the "public philosophy." In his book *The Public Philosophy*, Lippman, quoting Ernest Barker, says (paperback, p. 81f.):

> For over two thousand years European thought has been acted upon by the idea that the rational faculties of men can produce a common conception of law and order which possesses a universal validity.

This natural law or law of human rational nature, Lippmann continues, is a rational order of human society "in the sense that all men, when they are sincerely and lucidly rational, will regard as self-evident" (p. 95).

The American and French revolutions at the end of the eighteenth century, and the political regimes they established, were among the best fruits of these assumptions of rationalism. In the nineteenth century the assumptions came to be questioned and even, in many quarters, rejected. One of the major problems of contemporary political theory is the rehabilitation of this old basis or the discovery of a satisfactory new one. Walter Lippmann wrote the book we have quoted as an attempt at rehabilitation.

2.26 The "Axiom" of the State-Contract: Individualism

One of the supposedly self-evident axioms of this rationalistic political thought was the doctrine of the state-contract. This meant that the political order could be reduced to "free individual acts, to a voluntary contractual submission of the governed", in what they took to be their own interest. Here there is no idea of a corporate society to which God has given offices, but a collection of equal individual rational men. Here there is no idea of a service of God and an administration in His name, of the whole earth, but only a contractual agreement in the interest of the contracting individuals. (This is undoubtedly the deepest religious reason for the development of modern politics as "*belangenpolitiek*," a politics of self-and group-interests.) In this theory of contract, we see the *individualism* of the rationalist political theory. It is not so that the Law-word of God has laid down in the Order of Creation a typical state-structure with its own (delegated and limited) authority, and that we men were created to this and other law-structures. In the beginning, according to the theory, there are only individual men, who then contract together, in their own interest, to live together in a political community. The Law-word that constitutes the State a possibility lies in the rational root-life of each thinking individual.

2.27 Also Faith in Basic Community

At the same time, on the ground of the supposed (axiomatic) commonness of Reason, there was in this individualistic outlook the possibility of community. The very self-evidencing character of the principial or innate concepts of the common Reason compels a common acknowledgment. This common acknowledgment of what each thinking man, by thinking back (properly) to the roots of his thought, is sure to find as his own deepest Light and Truth, assures true community among all right-thinking men.

Here again we feel the religious motive at work in rationalism's rapid conquest of the hearts of western men. By the seventeenth century the – at least apparent – unity of European society had been as good as destroyed. Concord and unity are a matter of religion. When God opens the hearts of men to give heed to His Will, a unanimity (literally, oneness of heart: Greek, *homonoia*; Latin, *Concordia*) results, viz. the will to do the Father's (revealed) Will. The unity of men is achieved in their single-hearted devotion to one Law. Our unity and concord here on earth has a supra-historical origin in the Kingdom of God: with the divine opening of the heart the mind of Christ the Head is formed in all the members of the Body.

Pagan thinkers of ancient times never had such a clear insight into the relation between our whole life-in-this-world and its supra-historical root in the religious relation to God and His Law. Yet writers like Aristotle and Cicero realized that a truly stable society is impossible where there is dissension or discord, not, of course, about trivial matters, but about ultimates, specifically, about the supreme or ultimate authority or power in society. Ortega y Gasset has written: "Concord implies a firm and common belief regarding the exercise of supreme power." In the State, which to the ancients, as we saw last year, was the all-encompassing bond of society, there had to be agreement on fundamentals, and such agreement was guaranteed by religious sanction. Various Olympian deities sealed the authority of the several Greek city-states; the old Roman religion secured a common belief in the authority of the Roman Republic.

When the common belief no longer is there, a crisis of the foundations ensues. Such a crisis arose in the time of Cicero: belief in the old religion of the Romans was gone, and with it the basis for stability in the life of the state. What happens in a society when a firm belief in the ultimate sovereignty has been lost? Cicero asked himself the question. Society *requires* the executive function. Lacking a genuine solution, she resorts to a *makeshift*. Such a makeshift was the Roman Empire. A balancing of forces, of rival human wills.

2.28 Need for Community in Early Modern Europe

In the sixteenth century, after the anti-Christian humanism of the Italian Renaissance, the Reformation had brought an end to any commonness of faith that still lingered in Europe as to the ultimate authority. Since practically all the men of the time were committed to the axiom that there had to be an agreement on fundamentals if there were to be a stable society, the bitter struggles that took place between the forces of the Reformation and the Roman Church and Empire are thoroughly understandable. Each group, convinced of the truth of its position, was out to gain the common consent of Europeans. When this proved impossible, resort was had to another makeshift: the Religious Peace of Augsburg of 1555, by which the Lutheran religion was given legal status within the Empire, the principle of *cuius regio eius religio* was recognized, and subjects were granted the privilege of emigrating without molestation. This makeshift accentuated the local autonomy of the princes and thus contributed to the further breakdown of the Empire.

Men who thought fundamentally about the European situation realized that a mechanical balance of forces was not the solution to the question of European stability. But what to do? Meanwhile, the Calvinists, who had rapidly increased in number and counted many energetic leaders in a number of important towns, were not recognized in the "solution" of 1555. The Wars of Religion which broke out were followed by the Peace of Westphalia of 1648. This treaty confirmed the Religious Peace of Augsburg of 1555 and extended its provisions to the Reformed Churches. Toleration was now secured for the three great religious communities of the Empire. Within these limits the governments were bound to allow at least private worship, liberty of conscience and the right of emigration.

2.29 Rationalism's Community of Reason Meets the Need

This Peace of Westphalia remained the basis of European public law until the outbreak of the French Revolution. The toleration granted by it was of the old kind, but henceforth persecution, even of groups not recognized in the treaty, was the exception rather than the rule. A principal reason for this tolerant execution of its provisions was not just that men were growing weary of the struggle; it was something much more positive. Almost imperceptibly men's minds had been growing more tolerant. This tolerance was the expression of a *new outlook* on the world which was rapidly winning followers, especially among cultural leaders in the early decades of the seventeenth century. Leibniz, one of the greatest thinkers of the age, tried all his life to find a basis for the reunion of the several Christian communities, but to no avail. It was beginning to appear as though an order of universal agreement, so necessary for a stable society, could no longer be based upon a common confession of Christian dogma. Many leading thinkers were coming to the conviction that if there was to be a really universal system of law, ethics, or religion, it would have to be based upon such principles as could readily be acknowledged by every nation, creed and sect. The ancient theory of universal and necessary truths of reason, a form of the natural law theory, offered itself. In their great need men fell upon it as upon a saviour. The universally acceptable principles that were needed as the common foundation for European culture were now asserted – quite dogmatically, it would have seemed, had it not had such a long history – to be the *a priori* possession of every man in his rational life. War was principially abolished. Peace and community would certainly be found.

2.30 The Modern Rationalistic Mind

By this time it is possible for us to see how fundamental a thing this theory of rationalism is in the history of modern western man. It is so fundamental an "idea" that it leads to a reconstruction (revolution) of European society in its entirety. In the concept of Reason man assures himself with respect to the two basic (and related!) needs of *certainty* and *community*. Conceived as having his most essential roots in this Ratio, man is the sovereign possessor of Truth; indeed, in his deepest self he is the Truth, and thus cannot be estranged from it. (That is how the later theme of the self-estrangement or self-alienation of man, to be found already in Hegel, acquires extraordinary poignancy.) He is basically at home in a world that yields up its secrets to rational penetration. There is no need of salvation; man is right with the world. And, as to the future, he is wholly confident of his gradually increasing control of his environment by means of rational-technical techniques. It is just a question of working out the details. Rationalistic man is optimistic. Continual innovation and endless experimentation are the way to mastery. There is no *revelatory* Light of a Creation-order. There is no Order to which he was created. Reason, as original Light, can ignore any question as to a Light of Creation. It generates its own Order out of itself as *creative thought*. It *makes* its world. Being always and everywhere the same, it will – ultimately produce One World. The Kingdom of blessed souls, i.e. the Kingdom of good or right-thinking men is assured if only we act in accordance with reason. Proceeding by its light, men will progress onwards and upwards until they achieve a *natural*, earthly and common City of Man. The universal community. There is no place in this rationalism for a deep, fundamental Antithesis of direction in human life, – only for Community. Christ and the Holy Spirit's work have been made superfluous. There is no thought here of Christ's returning to put down the enemy and set up His Kingdom. The possibility of community resides not in a conversion and common obedience to Christ, but in a working out of our commonly shared rationality. Here we have the background for the faith that so many of our contemporaries have in the salutary consequences of shared beliefs, democratic discussion, the Town Meeting. When Franklin Roosevelt went to Yalta to talk with Stalin, he felt assured that if only emotion and historically arisen misunderstandings (prejudice) could be cleared up, rational analysis would reveal to all participants commonly, the truth of the situation, all rational men would be governed by the light of that truth, and a world-community of nations might then be erected.

2.31 Antithetical Religious Nature of Modern "Mind"

If all this is involved in the new "mind" of the seventeenth and eighteenth centuries, we can well understand the enthusiastic processions to the "shrine" of the goddess of Reason that characterized the hey-day of the French Revolution. And we can now see why I said earlier that this Revolution can serve, not only as a point of orientation, but as a *kind of norm* for fixing the meanings of the two political movements of the last two centuries. For then the French Revolution is indeed fundamentally the breaking out into the open, every day, practical life of mankind of man's *religious* abandonment in his heart of the Law of God and his substitution for that of the law of his own creative rational thought. Then Burke and Groen van Prinsterer are right that the Revolution has crucially to do with the radical religious direction of man's life on earth. Only such an estimation of it can adequately account for the very peculiar fascination it has for so many men.

As an *"omkering der goddelijke orde"* – an overturning of the divine Order – it reveals itself as Revolution in the *religious sense*, a revolution against the Law and Order of God, against the Rule of Christ, against the witness of the Holy Spirit, – in short, against the scriptural revelation of the Truth. This deeply religious character of the modern revolutionary mind – which also breaks down the accumulated everyday experience in order to rebuild in an abstract and unhistorical way, and in this way too discloses a revolutionary character (something we discussed last year in the lecture "Scientific and Pre-scientific," see particularly p. 19 top), and against which the Historical School of nineteenth century jurisprudence came up in so violent a reaction – thus presents itself to us as an effort at articulating, in the way of antithetical distortion, the Thesis of God. God's Thesis is our Norm; this evil thing that arises in the "imaginings" of man's heart, seen in the light of the Thesis as a distortion wrought by the deceptions of that old and First Rebel, the Devil, offers itself as *a kind of norm*. In this way we can fix the religious meaning of the political movements of the modern world.

2.32 Out of the Revolution Three Attitudes Emerge

All of you are familiar with the story of the French Revolution. It is so very fundamental that we must constantly return to it. How the "glorious" revolutionary which marched onwards and upwards in the name of the goddess of Reason so very quickly turned into the blood-bath that is known as the Reign of Terror. We cannot here take the time to describe this sudden and horrible metamorphosis. Important to note at present is that the Terror forced men to render an account of what had happened. And so, it came about that out of the fierce and torturous revolutionary events, a number of distinct human attitudes towards them emerged, which we must now seek to describe.

2.33 The Consistent Believers

There were, first, the *consistent believers*. Some men, beholding the blood-bath in all its hideousness, continued in a straight course, determined. They believed fully in their Cause, which was that, religion, and specifically the Christian religion, had been a bad superstition that had held men back from that complete scientific mastery of the conditions of their existence which would bring peace and blessedness on earth. They wanted to free themselves utterly from their past enslavement to such bonds and give themselves whole-heartedly to the task of self-redemption. They could do it in the power of Reason. Reason would show the way to humanity's unbelievably glorious future. But then they had to follow its demands. They *had to be consistent, no matter what.* Those who had learned how best to apply their rational powers to the conquest of the environment were the ones who spoke with Reason's own authority; they were rationalism's leaders (a distortion of the idea of "office").

Suppose now, for a moment, that you really believe this rationalistic theory, and that you are yourself one of the elite in rational-technical thought and planning, one of the brain-trust. How will you act when the weal or woe of mankind depends upon the rational decision you, as elite-thinker, must make at a specific moment of history, at that moment when, as it seems, all eternity concentrates its weight of meaning upon you and you are, as it were, infinitely aware that your decision involves the salvation or destruction of the human race. You are the expert, do not forget, the only one who has rationalized all the factors and knows what the situation really is. And now you *make* your decision. It is, without doubt, the path prescribed by Reason; it is the Law-word. But then some insignificant peasant or working-man stands up in a political gathering somewhere and says: But we do not want that; we want to be free to go our own way. And now you know, the thought expert who have thoroughly analyzed the situation rationally, that the course desired by your impertinent little opponent would be disastrous, something like genocide or race-suicide. How will you look upon this resistant person? Why, he is clearly a threat to all mankind. Such a reaction on the part of a really believing rationalist is understandable. The thought-experts will think to themselves: But we have studied all the factors involved. We alone can see what the situation is and requires. If these people do not follow us, they will destroy themselves. So, they have got to follow us. And if they will not, off with their heads!

2.34 Their Abstract Idealism

It is not that the rationalist elite are wicked murderers. Indeed, in the French Revolution some of those responsible for the Terror were men of a very high calibre and of noble sentiment. But they were at the same time without any compassion and unrelenting because they believed that Principle governs life, and the true Principle had to be made to prevail. They, the elite of Reason, had by their rational analysis and technical planning to make the world safe for all its inhabitants. The uninformed and willful masses would have to be compelled to obey the clear dictates of Reason. After all, the *salus* of all the people, even of all peoples, is at stake. And so they proceed to cut off heads. Out of a single-hearted devotion to their Principle. Mind you, out of (a somewhat abstract, to be sure!) *love for all mankind.*

We ought never to overlook this idealistic motivation of many believers in the rationalist Cause. I am confident, for example, that many believers in communism have experienced just such a motivation. The fact is repeatedly witnessed to by those who later "lost faith," as, for instance, Whittaker Chambers in his deeply stirring book *Witness.* When we render an account of the horrible deeds of the revolutionaries we must not play this feature short. Dostoevski has written a number of times about the destructive and even criminal possibilities of reason. "In *The Possessed* a group of political intellectuals are shown as being possessed by devils, ready to scheme, lie, even kill for the abstract ideals of Progress, reason, socialism" (Barrett, *Irrational Man*).

2.35 Their Revolutionary Concept of Freedom

These radical believers in the Cause of the Revolution were on their way. (The modern idea of Progress.) They would liberate themselves from the superstition and the fetters that had restrained them in the past and go on to freedom – no laws except ones that were freely self-imposed in their self-calculation of their self-interest – in the dawning Age of Man. There was no revelatory Law-order of Creation (e.g. sphere-sovereignty) already there, to which they were made, which would guide them in their acts; the world was a thoroughly *open* world and endless experimentation was the free route to travel. There is no law-structure of marriage, no family, no seven-day week rooted in the Will of God. Try communes, a ten-day week, state-regulated cohabitation. This is the mentality that most recently characterized the Chinese Revolution. It seems to have been as *true* there as it has always been in previous revolutions! The revolutionaries are always engaged in an effort against the structure of reality, but this also always holds them back. God maintains His Truth. They are restrained by the divine Law-order, also in the "offices" which Christ maintains. The revolutionaries do not know and love the Truth that to be free is to be redeemed from the deceptions of that old Rebel, Satan, and to live to God in terms of the Law He posited for us and to which He made us. They seek "freedom," and find themselves everywhere in chains. Humiliated and defeated, they stand up again and struggle on. They want, above all, to be "free." Sometimes such "believers" are not far from the Gospel of the Kingdom. As Christians, we ought to have a significant word for them and not pass them by.

2.36 The "Resigned" Believers

Besides the radical or confident believers there was a second group, whose attitude to the Terror comes down to something like this: the idea of the Revolution is all right, but we simply cannot stand all that bloodshed. This group did not object to the principles of the Revolution, but only to the *speed and thoroughness* with which the confident believers proceeded to carry them out. They wanted to travel in the same direction, but at a slower pace. They were less thoroughly abstract in their logic, and more ready to accommodate themselves to the requirements of the immediate situation. They might be called *resigned* believers. They were outspokenly for "freedom," and for them too freedom meant breaking the bonds that in the past had held them subject to traditional "spiritual" and "secular" authority, and building a future on the foundation of rational enlightenment. At heart, then, they were progressivists: having, as a first thoroughly enlightened generation, broken the hold that past superstitions and prejudices had had upon them, they could not look to the past for any guidance, but only to an entirely open future of new construction, innovation, novelty. Progress was the new that would come. Only, the Program was not to be so ruthlessly carried out; to ensure success, the leaders of the Revolution would have to reckon more concretely with the existing situation. These were the Moderates or Liberals of the Revolution.

2.37 The Conservative Reaction

A third reaction to the violence of the Revolution criticized the fundamental ideas of the revolutionary movement, but it did not criticize them fundamentally enough. The men who shared this general point of view represent a number of traditions and hold the common position for varying reasons. What they had in common was a fear of the abstract reasoning of the revolutionaries, of the levelling tendency of their ideas, of their radical rejection of the (unenlightened) past in favour of innovation and the new. These men were opposed to innovation-*ism*, to progressiv*ism*. They wished to conserve the values of the past, the traditional societal order, the established ways. Some were largely opportunistic conservatives, who desired above all to hold on to their inherited lands and wealth, their positions of privilege. But many really believed in an Order that is previous to our doing. A large part of the group was undoubtedly made up of those who still, albeit vaguely, represented the old synthetic idea of medieval Christendom, passed down in England, for example, in the influential writings of Richard Hooker. The weakness that characterizes all synthesis thought is the weakness of this group. No attempt is made to bring the integral Light of the Thesis to bear upon the antithetical religious origin of the revolutionary ideas. They speak of the Finger of God in history, of Design, even of Providential operation in the slow grinding out of the mill of history. But along with Christians who in their own minds may be thinking somehow of the God of the Scripture there are others who are thinking in terms of Aristotle's hierarchy of "forms" or of Plato's realm of purely intelligible essences, or of the Stoic cosmic logos, – in other words, of an *intelligible* world-order. It is just the synthesis which attempts a fusion of these antithetical Greek philosophical constructions with the scriptural revelation of God's Law-order. When this group refers to God and the "finger of God" or Providence it means to satisfy both Christians and the men of the ancient Greek ways of thinking. Just as you see it in Thomas Aquinas. An intellectual order of the natural world, modelled after Plato and Aristotle, *and* the revelation that there is an Order of Creation, *but then the latter understood in the sense of the former*. It is this attitude of synthesis that precludes conservatism's ever becoming a genuinely Christian political movement that could prove so influential, even decisive, in our troubled time. For, fundamentally, conservatism, like the rationalistic mind of the seventeenth and eighteenth centuries which it professes on so many points to despise, shares with it the fear of a religiously divided cultural life. It must therefore appeal to *reasonable* men, and thus does not get to the bottom of the crisis of our culture.

Here, briefly sketched, we have the three basic attitudes that emerged clearly from the holocaust of the French Revolution: the confident believers, often called the Radicals, who determined the original *direction* of political life in the new revolutionary age; the moderate progressivists or liberals (*de Gematigden*), who followed along in the same principial direction but more gradually, accommodating themselves more to existing circumstances; and the conservatives, who saw more in the past that ought to be conserved and accordingly reacted against the abstract innovationism of the revolutionaries.

2.38 A Contemporary Historian's Analysis

This is essentially the analysis that Groen van Prinsterer made already in the 1830's. To show you that it is not just the view of a nineteenth century Dutch Reformed Christian, let me refer you to one of our most outstanding cultural historians in the United States, the Harvard historian, Crane Brinton, who says substantially the same thing. This statement of his occurs in his excellent book *Ideas and Men*, p. 410. (The section of this book that deals with the modern period was reprinted separately in an inexpensive paper-back entitled *The Shaping of the Modern Mind*. The passage I am now referring to is to be found on p. 146 of it.) Here is the statement.

Into the course of the French Revolution – which was in its repercussions Western, not merely French – we cannot enter here. To its makers, as well as to its enemies, it was a proving-ground for the ideas of the Enlightenment. Here the experiment of abolishing the old bad environment and setting up the new good environment was actually made. The experiment produced the Reign of Terror, Napoleon, and a bloody war. Obviously, something had gone wrong. Yet the intellectual leaders of mankind by no means drew the simple conclusion that the ideas behind the experiment were wholly wrong. They drew indeed many conclusions, and from these conclusions much of the nineteenth and twentieth century is understandable. We shall in the following chapters make a very rough division into those who, though shocked by the Revolution, continued to hold, with the kind of modifications suited to respectable middle-class people, the basic ideas of the Enlightenment; those who attacked these ideas as basically false; and those who attacked these ideas, at least as incorporated in nineteenth-century society, as basically correct, but distorted, or not achieved, or not carried far enough. Putting the matter in terms borrowed from politics, we shall consider the points of view of Center, Right, and Left.

Brinton puts the party which gradually gained the upper hand in political life, the Moderates, in the center, the Radicals to the left, and the Conservatives to the right. This is common practice. As you can see, the agreement with Groen's analysis made one hundred years earlier, is striking!

2.39 America Swept into the Revolutionary Stream

Many American Christians continue to believe that the United States of America is essentially a Christian land, and that the revolutionary movement we have been describing has had little, if any, influence there. I can only say that this is not the case. Already I have referred to the influence of John Locke and the deists upon Voltaire. Their influence upon the American Founding Fathers is also well-known. No single man has had more influence upon political thought in the United States than Locke. Actually, he has been more influential here than in England. Moreover, Crane Brinton, in the paperback mentioned above (p. 21), speaks of the eighteenth-century view of life, modified as it has been in the last two centuries, as "still at bottom our view of life, especially in the United States," and again writes (ibid, p. 139) that we Americans are now the chief heirs and representatives of what he calls "the world-attitude" of the Enlightenment. William Barrett too certainly is correct when in his book *Irrational Man* (p. 241f.) he says that the "two chief contestants in the present international situation are both rooted in the Enlightenment" in so far as they "reflect any general conception of man." Of America, in particular, he writes that "it was founded in the eighteenth century in the very heyday of the Enlightenment, and by men who participated in the clear rationality of that period." His conclusion is that "what the American has not yet become aware of is the shadow that surrounds all human Enlightenment." I could call Cassirer to witness, and a host of others of our best historians. Let me simply refer to a highly significant article which appeared in *Fortune* magazine, the issue of February, 1951. The main article of this issue begins on p. 68 and carries the pregnant title, "The American Proposition: A Permanent Revolution in the Affairs of Men." Permanent revolution, – that is, according to *Fortune* magazine, the meaning of America. The writer of the article says that "the U.S.A. represents a revolution in human affairs which had been in preparation for many hundreds of years, but which was actually undertaken in the eighteenth century and has been carried on ever since." He describes this revolution as one "of the human individual against all forms of enslavement; against all forms of earthly power, whether spiritual, political or economic, that seek to govern man without consulting his individual will."(!) He says that:

> in this revolution is a proposition we call the American Proposition for the reason that it is to be found most succinctly stated in the writings and speeches of the founders of this country. But in the eyes of those founders it was not merely a proposition for Americans; it was universal: a proposition for mankind, signalizing not merely an American revolution but a human revolution.(!)

2.40 The Permanent Revolution

The same article speaks of the American Revolution as the permanent revolution (continual progressive experimentation), and the writer suggests that this phrase was an invention of Leon Trotsky's. But allow me to quote from Groen van Prinsterer, who in 1860 in his brochure "*Le Parti Anti-revolutionnaire et Confessionnel dans l'Eglise Reformee des Pays-Bas*" declared (I quote from the Dutch translation of Mej. A. J. Dam, published by Oosterbaan en Le Cointre N.V., Goes, 1954, p. 67):

> Hoe echter kunnen zij – his Christian friends – vergeten,... dat de omverwerping op godsdienstig, staatkundig en maatschappelijk gebied, dat niet een tijdelijke omwenteling, maar een toestand, een revolutionnaire stand van zaken, dat de permanente Revolutie het onvermijdelijke gevolg is geweest en blijft van de loochening der afhankelijkheid van den mens ten opzichte van... God...[1]

This is Groen, in 1860. In the light of the Thesis, the Word of God, Groen "saw" what was transpiring, and was able to provide real insight into, and analysis of, the true situation. This is the situation in the very heart of which Americans too find themselves placed. It is the prevailing situation universally in our western world. If only Christians throughout the western world had listened one hundred years ago to Groen, the prophet!

2.41 Evaluation of Radicals and Liberals

After the first stage of the Revolution had run its course, the

---

1. [English Translation] "But how can they forget... that the overturning in the religious, the political and the social areas, that not a temporary revolution but a condition, a revolutionary state of affairs, *that the permanent Revolution* was and remains the inescapable consequence of the denial of the dependence of man upon... God..."

direction of western political life fell largely to the Liberals or Moderates, to whom the Radicals or confident believers appeared extremists. Accordingly, today most people think of the Left – e.g. socialism and communism – as the extreme party. It is wholesome, therefore, to have Groen remind us, as he does in his famous book *Ongeloof en Revolutie* (*Unbelief and Revolution*) that the group we thus call extremists is really the party of faith, the men who believed that Principle directs life and had the courage to live by their faith. In this connection it is interesting to notice that Whittaker Chambers in *Witness* speaks of the communists as the only segment of mankind that can still bring up a measure of faith. (Here then is the one outstanding exception to the prevailing apathy. But where are the Christians!?!) The Liberals, on the other hand, though in agreement with the principial direction of the Revolution, hesitated, compromised, accommodated, adjusted their course of action, in their own – often quite material – interest. These Liberals have taught us, who live in a history they in general have moulded, to believe that the Revolution went wrong because of the *excesses* of the Radicals. Groen the Christian makes clear – and it is a fundamental matter to get straight – that it is not the excess that was wrong, but the essential revolutionary *direction* of events. The "principium" heralded by the revolutionaries is not the Principium of life; it is an antithetical distortion. To follow its leading, in whatever tempo, can only lead to a sickening of society and its ultimate destruction, except for the intervention of God, Who always maintains His Thesis and restrains the destruction of the wicked.

Groen had respect for the Radicals of the Revolution to the extent that they were *believers*. They had seen something of the real structure of life. Their influence was destructive because they had a false and abstract belief. They had put their faith in an abstractly conceived Reason, an idol, *afgod, onding*. The Liberals, to be sure, moved generally forward in the same revolutionary stream, but their adjustments out of so-called practical and utilitarian considerations made them appear more "*zakelijk*" (business-like) and tended to obscure the driving religious principle that was yet operative in the course of events.

2.42 The Radical Danger of Liberalism

The merit of Groen's prophetic insight was that he could utter the forceful warning that the same destruction that radicalism brings with it is also inherent in liberalism. His illuminating and manifestly correct analysis can be very briefly reproduced in two statements he quotes from his German statesman-friend Stahl, in *Ongeloof en Revolutie* (*Unbelief and Revolution*), ed. Smitskamp, p. 170, note 24:

> The democratic [a word frequently used a hundred years ago for the Radicals – H.E.R.] party, which is described by its liberal opponents as *the party of anarchy*, offers a criticism of the liberal party that is correct. But this proper criticism, which it directs to the liberals, does not yet make it itself a correct party. On the contrary, since it is itself a more thorough and more energetic application of the principle of the revolution it is also a worse and more pernicious error than the liberal party. To be sure, there is nothing good in half-heartedness and irresolution, but the consistent form of the error is even worse than a half-hearted embrace of it.

To this first statement of Stahl, Groen appends the remark that while this is so, we must at the same time keep in mind that those who embrace the principle of the revolution inconsistently (the Liberals) are actually preparing the way for that very end-result which they loathe. Here he quotes Stahl a second time: "I am not afraid of the *acute* sickness of democracy [radicalism – H.E.R.]; I am afraid of the *chronic* sickness of liberalism. I do not fear *radical revolution*, but rather the *gradual dissolution*." If I may add a witness of my own, I think that we Christians today ought to ponder over these words for a long time. In what direction is our political life slowly pulling us *over the years?*

2.43 Extension of Revolutionary "Mind"

Although during the nineteenth century radicalism remained a peripheral movement – e.g. Saint-Simon, Fourier, Proudhon, Herzen, Russian populism –, gradually the scope of influence of the revolutionary ideas was considerably enlarged. After the French revolution the struggle between the classes began anew in Switzerland, which was now so stimulated by the French example that the object was no longer merely to regain ancient popular rights, but to introduce the new abstract "equality" and "fraternity." The year 1798 even saw the complete overthrow of the Swiss constitution and the establishment of the Helvetic Republic. With the subsequent revolutions of 1830 and 1848 the secularistic mind of liberalism was brought down to the great masses of workers, who, as a result of the Industrial Revolution and its injustices, were beginning to find their collective voice. To the conservatives fell the extremely heavy task of attempting to stem the revolutionary tide. In this way the political landscape of the nineteenth century came to be dominated by the two figures of liberalism and conservatism.

2.44 Liberalism vs. Conservatism

So enthralled had western men become by this whole onrushing spectacle that the choice between the progressivism of the liberals and the conservatives' (originally) firm rejection of the shallow and abstract "Reason" of the Enlightenment for the accumulated wisdom of the ages, fixed in prescription and prejudice, tradition and habit, could not but appear to be the most fundamental choice with which they would be confronted. This point of view the twentieth century has inherited (but in a somewhat modified form yet to be described). The political disjunction, the political alternative, the radical choice in political life is said to be liberalism versus conservatism.

2.45 This Not the Basic Alternative

Earlier in this lecture I ventured to suggest that the contrast between conservatism and liberalism or progressivism is never to be identified with the radical (religious) difference in direction which there really is in human life, and which, in a wholesome historical development, will have to come to a *political articulation*. In the cultural mandate, which, as part of the divine Law for life, defines our task in the world, there is both a conserving and a dynamic or progressive element. Adam was commanded to keep the garden and to dress it. Conservation and progress are not alternative choices of a disjunction (which together exhaust the possibilities and are mutually exclusive); they are, in fact, *complementary* aspects of the integral human Task. (We shall see in a moment that the organization of political life into the two parties or movements of conservatism and liberalism has led finally to the frank statement that they are complementary to each other.)

We saw, further, that in order for these two terms to be meaningful they must be seen in relation to a norm which is above them both, viz. the Law of God which declares what is good and what is evil. With respect to progress the crucial question is not the impatient one of the revolutionaries about how quickly we are advancing, but whether we are advancing *in the good direction.* Not all change is improvement or progress. There is an Order of Creation to direct us, the knowledge of which is republished in the Gospel of Jesus Christ. An increasing measure of obedience to this revealed Will of our Creator-Redeemer, so that the purpose of Christ's coming into the world and of our living in it as agents of His work of reconciliation is achieved, viz. that all things be brought back to a right relation to the Father – we talked about it in our first lecture –: this is true progress, or the good in its progressive aspect. On the other hand, the old that has come down to us out of the past is neither wholly good nor completely evil. Repeatedly in my lectures here at Unionville I have pointed out to you that the religious obedience and disobedience of past generations, and the effect of the witness and restraint of God, are worked into the form-giving of the traditional ways and institutions, the prescriptions and prejudices we inherit and pass on. The forms of our institutions and organizations express a belief about the nature of our life and how its problems are to be tackled and solved. This inherited past must prophetically be judged in the light of the Norm (Thesis). Prof. Vollenhoven sums up the matter quite neatly in a lecture he recently deliv-

ered at the Free University of Amsterdam entitled "Conservatisme en Progressiviteit in de Wijsbegeerte" and which is to be
found in the volume of "interfacultaire colleges" given at the
university in 1958 and published under the title *Conservatisme
en Progressiviteit in de Wetenschap* by Kok of Kampen in 1960.
(I quote the article because it is a little jewel, and I hope all of
you who can read it will.) To look at this matter of conservatism and progressivism in the light of the norm of the central
divine Law of love, Vollenhoven writes, is to see

> dat we in het kwade niet mogen berusten, op hoe hoge ouderdom
> het ook kan bogen of in welke ongekend nieuwe glans het zich aan
> ons voordoet, en… dat we ons in den strijd voor het goede niet onbe-
> tuigd laten, ook al zou het aanvankelijk en bij conservatieven en
> bij progressieven nauwelijks aandacht trekken.[2]

2.46 But It Explains Sacrosanctity of Two-Party System

We have now seen how it came about that, when in the course
of the nineteenth century the possibility of sharing in the determination of the direction of the life of the state was opened
up to the newly awakened masses of men, the organization of
political life fell, except for the more or less peripheral radical
movements, into the two supposed directions of liberalism and

---

2.   [English Translation] "that we may not resign ourselves to or acquiesce
     in that which is evil, no matter with what claims to hoary antiquity it
     may come to us or in what unprecedentedly new halo of glory it may
     present itself to us, and . . . that in the struggle for that which is good
     we are not to leave ourselves without a witness even though at first it
     might scarcely draw the attention of either conservatives or progres-
     sives."

conservatism. At a certain pregnant moment in the history of western man this choice appeared on the political horizon as the decisive and radical choice of mankind. This explains the feeling of high regard for the two-party system and its ideal desirability, a feeling that frequently comes close to acknowledging its sacrosanctity. We ourselves know that this choice is not the radical choice between good and evil. But we may not acquiesce in this situation by saying that there is evil everywhere in this life and nothing is an unmixed good. The matter is a question of *principle*. (A proposed third or "middle way" does not help; such a "mean" is thoroughly defined by the two "extremes," which in this case are not genuine extremes.) Here a number of observations remain to be made.

2.47 Further Analysis of Liberalism

In the first place, the liberalism which generally gained the upper hand in the direction of political life was, as I have indicated, not a radical or consistent articulation of the antithetical religious commitment represented by rationalism. The liberals were not hearty believers; they were compromisers. They had rightly seen the destruction that had followed upon a whole-hearted acceptance of the pseudo-principle of "Reason." If they had drawn the conclusion that the principle of rationalism was an idol, nothing at all but a distortion of the Truth, they would have been on the right path. But this is not the true significance of the liberalistic movement in modern political life. The liberals offered no principial criticism of the faith of the radicals; they merely criticized the ruthlessness of execution. They wanted an orderly and quiet course of events, what someone has called the "*geruisloze revolutie*" (the silent revolution). These bourgeois capitalists, weaned from Christianity, imbibed the spirit of the Enlightenment. But they needed peace and rest for their business interests. They accommodated themselves to what they called the factual situation. They adjusted to the facts.

The liberals, without distantiating themselves from the principial direction of radicalism, became skillful adjusters. They said that they allowed the immediate factual situation to guide them. Of course – we saw it in the last lecture –, one can never understand the immediate "factual" situation except in the light of a Principle. And that is just what was lacking in liberalism. Recoiling from the consequences of living whole-heartedly by the light of the anti-principle or antithetical principle of the radical revolutionaries, they found nothing to take the place of the principle itself. Or rather, they attempt to allow the "facts" to take the place of a principle. At this point they are without direction, blind, drifting with the immediate so-called facts of everyday's concern for making a living. The liberals became opportunists. Supple, they like to call it. But it really means blind, and if God did not cause His Thesis to impinge with force also upon them, they would be utterly lost. The difficulty with their position is that the "factual" situation they talk about is a mixed thing religiously, into which the religious obedience and disobedience of past human behaviour is worked, and to make genuine progress out of this present miserable situation towards the glory of future salvation requires the direction of a Principle that is sure, so that we can "see" what we are to do and work truly *reformatorically*, to bring everything into subjection to the Rule of God in accordance with His holy Order of Creation. Liberalism does not reform according to the Norm, and that alone is our human calling. Rejecting the guidance of the Word of God, liberalism can offer no resistance to the antithetical pseudo-principle of the Revolution. Actually, to the extent that some guiding principle *must* be present, it is the principle of the modern rationalistic revolution. But at the same time its hideous revolutionary character is obscured under its "supple" living with the "facts" (which, by the way, the scientists will track down for us: scientism!). Liberalism pulls us constantly to the Left, without our becoming so very conscious of it. Groen was right in his fear of the "*geruisloze revolutie.*"

2.48 And of Conservatism

Likewise, the conservative movement, which had found its "antirevolutionary" voice in Edmund Burke (*Reflections on the Revolution in France*, 1790) and in a number of continental, frequently Roman Catholic, writers, was more able than liberalism to offer *principial resistance* to the gradual but constant revolutionary "drift to the Left." True, the conservatives were opposed to innovationism. They did not accept the levelling doctrine of the common "Reason"; they rejected the notion that there is no Order except that effected by the "ordering" *ratio*. But conservatism was unwilling to deal radically with the *religious root* of the Revolution.

2.49 Significance of Groen van Prinsterer

It was this that Groen van Prinsterer saw, and his prophetic insight and evangelical obedience elevate him above all the other conservatives of his time. It was what led him to break with conservatism. His act of evangelical obedience has given the Netherlands another political history in the nineteenth and twentieth centuries than the Anglo-Saxon countries. The difference is not a matter of national or racial differences; it is a difference in religious insight. In his religious insight Groen got beyond conservatism. His fundamental analysis can be summed up in one or two sentences: "Dat om de kwaal te verdrijven het niet voldoende is, de verschijnselen ervan te bestrijden, *maar de kiem moet worden weggenomen. Dat systematisch ongeloof slechts het geloof als tegengif heeft.*" (Italics mine. This citation is found in *De Antirevolutionnaire en Confessionele Partij in de Nederlands Hervormde Kerk*, p. 67f. Translation: "That to get rid of the evil it is not sufficient to combat its symptoms, *but the germ has to be removed. That the only antidote to systematic unbelief is belief.*" Radical and integral faith, we would say.)

2.50 Our Urgent Situation

The *principle* of rationalism was evil. There was need of *principial resistance*. This was needed in Groen's time; today there is scarcely a last chance for Christians to bring the Gospel of Jesus Christ in the political sphere. This is today a matter of the greatest urgency. It is a terrible thing that throughout the world theologians and "churchmen" very rarely show appreciation for this problem. Often their failure – for that is precisely what it is – is, I am convinced, to be written down to the fact that their training and traditional experience have influenced them to look upon the Word of God as a sourcebook for their theological judgments and ecclesiastical practice. All of us, if we are to have a powerful and redeeming word for our times, must rediscover the Word of God as the directing Principle of our whole life, in the sense that I have been explaining in my three series of Unionville lectures. In this manner our Unionville Conferences can be influential also in the renewing of our practical life (which, you remember, along with theory, is part of that life-*expression* which is directed to the service of God and the administration of the whole earth in His Name, both of these in terms of His Law-order, by the hold which the living and powerful integral Word of God gets upon our hearts). This is the larger significance of our conferences for Canada and, indeed, for the North American continent.

2.51 Powerlessness of Conservatism to Turn Tide

Conservatism sensed better than liberalism that the *principle* operative in the new political movement and driving it on in its course was a wrong principle. But conservatism was not in a position to reassert the Word of God in its integral revelatory sense as the only possible antidote. From the beginning the conservative political movement belongs to the modern world. Edmund Burke came out of a Whig background and had imbibed many notions of the prevalent humanism and "enlightenment." There was no thought of bringing to political articulation the religious split between acceptance of the Word of God as integral directing Principle of life and acceptance of an antithetical pseudo-principle. In Christian circles theologism, mysticism, and pietism had already greatly weakened whatever insight Christians had into the *scriptural* sense of the Word of God and the Christian religion. But, beyond that, conservatism was not a specifically Christian movement. This explains its *powerlessness to turn the religious direction political life had taken.*

Conservatism appealed to a rational or intelligible order that was visible in history, an order that *rational* man could deal with and talk about. Because Christians since the time of the earliest church fathers had, in an attempted synthesis of the (antithetically religiously directed) thought-results of the ancient classical peoples with the revelation of God in His Word, accepted Greek views about a rational order of "nature," they were unable to see the dangers of assuming a common political witness with unbelievers, and generally they joined in a movement with conservatives *against* the revolutionary movements. Unfortunately for the whole modern world, conservatism could not be genuinely "anti-revolutionary." Groen van Prinsterer, the confessor of the Gospel, was that, in principle.

Christians should have witnessed to the Order of Creation that is anchored in the Creator's Will (and republished in the Gospel), and to the divinely ordained (and revealed) "offices" in human life in which religious man in his three-fold office of prophet, priest, and king is called by God to "positivize" (give a positive form to, in history) the central Law of love for the various sectors of human life in the constantly changing circumstances. They would then have been compelled to break with the static, intellectualist-reductionist natural law theories and have brought a live, very relevant and urgently needed word (from the revelation of God) into the modern cultural discussion. For we need a sure Law that yet allows for dynamic historical development by man.

2.52 Relation of Conservatism to Historic Right School

But conservatism did nothing of the sort. Conservatism falls into an identification of the Order of God (which always remains Norm or Law *for* historical development, about which man in history must prophesy) *with what has developed in history*. Over against the abstract rationalistic thought-constructions of Voltaire, Rousseau and the famous *Déclaration des droits de l'homme et du citoyen*, Burke put the *organic growth* of English constitutional law and institutions. The conservative movement became closely allied with the Historic Right School of jurisprudence, which I mentioned last year in my lecture on sphere-sovereignty. "The founders of the Historic Right School," Cassirer tells us (*The Myth of the State*, paperback edition, p. 228), "declared that history was the source, the very origin of right. There is no authority above history". The rights of man are not those abstractly conceived "natural rights" of the revolutionaries, sanctioned supposedly by the *a priori* law-ideas of a "Reason" that is looked upon as the ultimate "ordering" authority. The conservative sees the sanction for the rights of men and of institutions and organizations in the *hoary antiquity* of these rights. The Law of God, which declares everywhere what is good and right, is drawn down into history and identified with the "finger of God," the gradual working out of the right in the development of history. The religiously responsible place of Office is brought down and identified with what in the course of history has acquired authority. Thus, the scriptural-religious view of reality has here, in fact, been reduced to a form of historical relativism. Whatever has established itself and gained recognition in the slow "growth" of history is right. Here we see a fundamental kinship to the "enlightened" view of the positive Tightness of all that is, the eighteenth-century notion of universal cultural evolution (optimism), especially with respect to the "offices" or historically established orders.

There is here no divine Law that is other than and above historical development, no deviation or religious apostasy of man working itself out in his positivizing labours in all the various areas of his life-activity, no need of religious *reformation* in all those areas by men whose hearts have been renewed, illumined and directed by the sovereign Word of God, who are restored in Christ to Office and the "offices." Is all historical change "organic growth"? Are there no *irreconcilable* conflicts in history, which express a *fundamental antithesis of religious direction* in human life? To put these questions here is sufficient to point up the anti-scriptural background of conservative thought.

2.53 Collapse in Historical Relativism

Having once taken his position within historical development, the conservative is lost. For history presents us with a continuous flux. At first, the conservatives, true to their criterion of *historically acquired rights*, defended the traditional orders and classes of European society, attempted to maintain, against the innovations of the new "purely rationally" conceived society, the old patriarchal conditions, society as an "organism." But straightway their real problem began to press them. If rights are historically acquired, what about the "rights" of the new revolutionary movement? This movement was gaining wide support among the rising industrial classes (because they too were either ignorant of or alienated from a scriptural view of their life), and had become consolidated in the time of Napoleon. How far would this historical development have to go, and how long would it have to prevail, before it too became integrated in the slow "growth" of history? In other words, how ancient is "hoary" ancient? How happy would the Christians who had attached themselves to the conservative movement have been with their conservative "ideology" in an Asiatic or African country where the Christian Church had no historically acquired rights, but cannibalism, say, did?

2.54 Deterioration of Conservatism

The conservative, unless he became more aware of the urgent need of a radically Christian answer to the problems involved, as Groen van Prinsterer did, in principle, in the Netherlands (though he too, as we saw last year, remained entangled *in his theoretical thought* in this Historic Right School, so that there was a conflict between his religious sensing of the situation and the inadequate theoretical structures by which he attempted to formulate what he sensed), could either fall back into a reactionary defense of the past, of already vested interests, and thus lose all genuine relevancy, have no significant view about the dynamic, the novel, in history; or he could find himself in the most unhappy position of following along after the more progressive accomplishments of the liberals (or more radical spirits), serving chiefly as a brake upon the dynamic movement of innovation. Especially as the power of the Christian faith waned in a quickly secularizing Europe and the belief in metaphysics (the old Greek views about an intelligible order, for instance, either free of or mixed with elements of biblical revelation) approached collapse, the position of conservatism came to be more and more that of a middle-road "take it easy" correction of the more vital course developed by the liberals. You can see now why the charge has been levelled (see earlier in this lecture) that "conservatism as an ideology lacks what might be termed a substantial ideal," i.e. a norm or principle of its own by which it can develop a distinctive standpoint; that the tag "conservatism" has been used to justify *any* existing order, at *any* stage of history; that one does not find in conservative circles any indication of the character of the political institutions and way of life conservatism as an ideology would be interested in defending.

2.55 Same Movements in America

We are now able to recognize the two movements of liberalism and conservatism as the climate of opinion in which the American Republic came into being. With respect to the American Declaration of Independence there were those more enlightened men around Jefferson who thought chiefly of their struggle with England in terms of the abstract reasoning of the Declaration's Preamble. But there were also men like John Adams who were concerned more with the "long train of abuses" the Declaration enumerates. Likewise, in attempting to formulate the sense of the American Revolution, some talked in terms of abstract "natural rights," but there were many conservatives like John Adams who defended the Revolution as a coming up for the rights of Englishmen, for ancient, historically acquired rights. Hence Adams' interest in the Declaration's enumeration of abuses. It is prophetic of the future significance of the American conservative movement that Adams *signed* the Declaration even though its tendency to the abstract "enlightened" theory did not represent his ideas on the meaning of the American Revolution. Already here we find conservatism, lacking any principial resistance, *being drawn to the left*.

2.56 Religious Criticism of Both Movements and of the Polar Structure

Everywhere in the world of modern political life we encounter this liberal-conservative polarity. Both movements represent a meaning that is pernicious because it is a falling away from the original Meaning of the Law-order of God's creation-Thesis. Liberalism tears "freedom" and "progress" out of their connection with man's responsible position in Office, where he is called to give new form to reality in the freedom of a whole-hearted subjection to the life-sustaining Law of God, and thus proclaims a destructive doctrine of *freedom*. Conservatism drags the religious Office of man down to historically arisen orders and establishments, and therefore presents us with a distorted and dangerous view of authority. Accordingly, neither of these two modern political movements can in any way be acceptable to Christians. But then it follows that the organization of the political life of a people in a national territory into this kind of polar structure is just as little acceptable. For the implied disjunction is not a proper one. Neither of the alternatives is correctly formulated, and there is another political position possible: a vigorous political articulation of the central religious knowledge of the divine Thesis that Christians have in Christ. A scripturally directed view of freedom and progress, of authority, of societal order and the limits of a political order (sphere-sovereignty), of the nature of community and of a genuine *political* community, of the correct manner of attempting a world-wide order of law in the light of the fundamental religious dividedness of the race, of the manner of voting and of day-by-day rule in a community fundamentally divided in its ultimate loyalties. Where Christians do not allow their *princip-*

ial protest to be heard against the present structuration of political life and make no attempt to articulate their own political faith, they can scarcely be said to be witnessing in their time and place. But then they can scarcely complain when they find it impossible to express themselves within the cultural forms of their times and thus find themselves squeezed out of the public life of the nation as *Christians*.

2.57 Further Deterioration of Liberalism

We have seen something already of the way in which conservatism deteriorated and became empty of meaning in the course of the nineteenth century. But liberalism, a compromise of bourgeois capitalists from the beginning, also underwent further deterioration. The collapse of faith in metaphysical constructions, which characterized the middle decades of the century, cooled whatever convictions men still held as to the capacity of "Reason" to direct their lives. In the further course of the century an awareness was dawning that men do not reason alike in all ages and places. Anthropological and ethnological investigations taught Europeans the relativity of rational insight. The Enlightenment belief in a common reason began to fade. But, with it, the religious strength of the revolutionary movement. It did not take long to draw the conclusion that if men's reasoning is different in different situations, it may not be an authoritative Director or Principle out in front (*a priori*) to guide us through life, but possibly part of our life-adaptation, a higher instrument of adaptation to a contingent physical environment. Where such a conclusion was drawn men were left without a guiding Principle (because their faith had been in an idol, an *onding*, a nothing) in a swirling world of factual states. This development brought the liberal movement too to a position of blind movement within factual situations that supposedly "said something" about how to act. And conservatism, which has also shared the effect of the above-sketched development, more and more drags along behind. We begin to understand the charge made by Stanley Knowles about the Tweedledum-Tweedledee character of conservatism and liberalism, and the contemporary phenomenon of political apathy (except among radical believers). Everybody just follows where the "facts" lead, moves as the "facts" dictate.

2.58 Complementarity Within a Common Rationality

Though they understood it differently, both movements had inherited the apostate-religious belief in the fundamental *oneness* of man's rational processes (the conservatives getting it generally from the medieval synthesis of Hellenistic teachings about *a priori* ideas with an interpretation of Romans 1 and 2, for example, in the light of those teachings). Now, both find themselves immersed in a supposedly "common factuality" which either speaks commonly to men or can be mastered by the application of a common technology, the traditionally liberal movement more progressively experimenting towards a new and *enlarged* freedom, the traditionally conservative group serving as a brake upon innovation and seeking to maintain the *established* order. The argument is frequently heard today that the two-party or two-movement system necessarily presupposes a fundamental commonness of commitment to ultimates, and that the two poles of our political life, instead of providing *radical alternatives*, should be thought of as *complementary* to each other. We need, it is then said, both bold experimentation and the maintenance of historical continuity, but on the background of a common fundamental belief. Walter Lippmann writes:

> For the toleration of differences is possible only on the assumption that there is no vital threat to the community. Toleration is not, therefore, a sufficient principle for dealing with the diversity of opinions and beliefs. It is itself dependent upon the positive principle of accommodation. The principle calls for the effort to find *agreement beneath the differences*" (*The Public Philosophy*, paperback edition, p. 132, italics mine).

2.59 Intolerance of Modern "Mind"

Here Lippmann can be seen signing the death warrant of those who would live radically and integrally by the powerful Word of the living God. Christianity will be tolerated where and only where it allows itself to be integrated with the rest of humanity's life. The confession that human life is characterized by a *fundamental* split of religious commitment is *intolerable*. The irony of the situation is that Lippmann derives hope for his rationalistic scheming from the long history of accommodation that is typical of the synthesis mind (see same book, p. 131). But what is the Christian believer to do? We are confronted here with the same old – and *fundamentally intolerant* – assertion of a *oneness* of the human race outside of a common submission to the Rule of Christ according to the Law-word of God. There is, to be sure, a oneness of the race apart from Christ: the concerted effort of men, for instance, to build the Tower of Babel (or a World United against the Rule of Christ). Against all such efforts the Christian must stand firm in order to save the race from self-destruction. Where, in Lippmann's view, may he stand – what room does he have the privilege (by Mr. Lippmann's favour) of occupying – in order to witness to the true Word of Christ about Community?

2.60 Fear of Wars of Religion

The fear of the old Wars of Religion can be seen behind the writing of many a contemporary writer. It is an indication of the unity of the so-called modern period of history that we are now coming back to the point at which the "modern" solution was initiated. Where Christians live by the Word of God those who are "without" need not fear for new religious wars. For Christians have themselves learned in the modern period that according to the Word of God the weapons they have as believers are the weapons of the Spirit, and the Word of God which is powerful to turn the "way" of men. The danger for humanity lies in the intolerance of radicalism, of liberalism (so-called) and a conservatism that sees itself as one pole of a united (monolithic) human race.

2.61 Some Deeper Insight in Our Time

Our times are getting more radical. That is, they are getting closer to the root of things. As, for example, when Karl Marx says, "To be radical is to go to the root of the question. Now the root of mankind is man." William Barrett (*Irrational Man*, p. 243) writes: "Behind the problem of politics, in the present age, lies the problem of man… anyone who wishes to meddle in politics today had better come to some prior conclusions as to what man is and what, in the end, human life is all about. I say "in the end" deliberately because the neglect of first and last things does not – as so-called "practical" people hope – go unpunished, but has a disastrous way of coming in the back door and upsetting everything. The speeches of our politicians show no recognition of this; and yet in the hands of these men, on both sides of the Atlantic, lies the catastrophic power of atomic energy."

2.62 Stark Reality of Antithesis

But the closer we get to the root of the political crisis of our times, the more we are made aware of the *root*-dividedness of our human race in its ultimate loyalty, its ultimate faith. There is an Antithesis in our life, and the belief in a race, fundamentally one in its confession of the Truth and the true Principle of life, is a *false belief*. No cultural articulation of such a false faith could ever be salutary for the race; it is not based on *realities*. But, meanwhile, as long as Christians try to live within the area of belief and action that western man decrees to be tolerable, our life will be constantly drawn in the direction of the final Catastrophe, the Destruction that is justly meted out to that oldest Rebel and his Revolution of Nihilism.

2.63 Groen's Criticism of an Irresponsible Individualism

In all this, is the Christian to stand idly by, accepting the place – pinched as it is – that modern man allocates to him, and watching his fellow-men prepare their own and also his earthly destruction? There were those in Groen's day who thought so, and Groen's words to them are just as applicable to us (*Ongeloof en Revolutie*, ed. Smitskamp, footnote 35 on p. 331f.):

We complain about Thorbecke [we might say, the democrats – H.E.R.], about the Lower House, and then about the modernists, and then about the Catholics, and then about anything else that might suggest itself, and we forget to complain about ourself, our own passivity, lukewarmness, cowardice. Upon us perhaps in double measure rests the reproach I made in the Lower House against the conservatives ... of being not "an active political party" but a wailing observer, always almost a mourning spectator, who does not exercise any influence upon the course of events that comes at him... I must call to your attention that the almost total lack of public spirit, of a sense of citizenship, that the indifference for public affairs with which the future of the Netherlands [*we* can substitute Canada or the U.S.A. – H.E.R.] is abandoned to unbelief [and revolution], that this trait of character, which characterizes Christendom generally in our day, is highly alarming and undeniably related to that egotism which is the constant enemy also of the Christian. We are, I have repeatedly said, here at home in state and church consumed by individualistic disparagement of the most simple demand of our patriotic and christian devotion to duty... Although we are not unjustly afraid of the *theory of individualism*, let us be especially on guard against the individualism of our own hearts.

Here Groen quotes de Tocqueville: "Individualism is a deliberate and peaceable feeling which makes every citizen inclined to separate himself from the mass of his equals and to withdraw indoors with his family and friends so that, after he has erected a little society for his own private use, he can without regret abandon society as a whole to its fate." To this Groen adds this telling sentence: "De vaderlandsliefde lost zich op in huisvaderlijk familiezwak," which is to say that we justify our abandonment of our political calling (as an integral aspect of our human Calling) by assuming, to an exaggerated and sickly degree, our obligations as the heads of our families.

2.64 Two Urgent Problems
1. How to Turn the Revolutionary Direction?

Two problems, it would seem to me, must at once have the attention of all of us who belong to Jesus Christ and would live by the Word of God. *First, how is the present revolutionary course of political development to be turned?* We have seen that there is actually but one 'principle' and one direction in modern political life. That direction is the direction that was originally given to it by the faith the Radicals of the Revolution had in the capacity of "Reason" to be the Principium of human life and society. The liberals travel, at a slower pace and perhaps in a more devious route, in the same revolutionary direction. The conservatives can at best delay the revolutionary development, although if they delay it by defending older evils and injustices, they only serve thereby to strengthen the desire of men for the progressive and wonderful new world of enlarged privilege. On the basis of a similar analysis Groen predicted already in 1845, three years before the publication of the *Communist Manifesto*, the advance in the West from liberalism to socialism to communism. No wonder the communists are confident about the future of the West!

How then can we get out from under this seemingly inexorable drift to the Left? By recognizing that it is no inevitable "historical necessity" but simply the articulation of an antithetical (and therefore false and destructive) pseudo-principle. We do not need large numbers of soldiers to combat the threat – they could not get at the root of the evil in any case –, but only a faithful and wholehearted witness of Christians to the Word of God as the true Principal of life. The Spirit of God, using the Word of God, can cause all the mighty political structures that emanate from a false principle to crumble and cave in like a pack of cards, by converting the *hearts of men* to the Truth. We must boldly place Principle over against "principle," and articulate for the political aspect of our lives the central religious knowledge we have in Christ. This is always a necessary, and in our time a highly urgent, part of our simple evangelical obedience.

2. How to Get Open Acknowledgement of Realities

The second problem confronting us Christians in the contemporary political world – and here we reach the deepest and most firmly entrenched root of the cancer, and the most dangerous moment of the (cultural) operation – is *how we are to get our contemporaries to see that for a vigorous political life there will have to be a free and open acknowledgement of the factual (religious) dividedness of the human race.* To achieve this we shall have to attempt to convince them that their own confidence in the oneness of the human community (i.e. *potential* oneness), rooted in a common rationality and/or a common experience, is not a necessary axiom of a Reason that is always and everywhere the same, nor a commonly felt pragmatic need, but nothing less than a religious faith which is in irresolvable conflict with a scripturally directed faith, and that one religious faith or another always gives direction, however hidden away from observation it may be, to all the life-activities of all men.

2.65 Common Task: Seek Proper Political Implementation

We have to do this in order to get our fellow men to the place where they will *search diligently with us for the proper political instruments or structures with which to implement this conviction*. For us Christians, this is only giving the necessary heed to the apostolic injunction that we must live, as far as possible, at peace with all men. The humanist should wish the same. The two-party or two-movement system, and what Arthur Schlesinger, Jr. has again called the "vital principle of republics," viz. absolute acquiescence in decisions of the majority (thus election by majority vote) – see his *The Age of Jackson*, paperback ed., p. 143 –, are actually implementations of a belief in the sovereignty of the people, who are also conceived as fundamentally at one, and whose political divisions will therefore always tolerate one another. But other forms of political life have been found – e.g. proportional representation – which allow Christians and others to live what they believe and still exist in the political community. As an example of what I mean, let me cite a significant passage from another book of Crane Brinton, *A Decade of Revolution: 1789-99*, p. 15:

> ...the two-party system may now be seen to have been an ideal generalization derived from certain dramatic moments of English and American history – the struggle between federalist and anti-federalist, the followers of Gladstone and those of Disraeli. Even in Anglo-Saxon countries the ideal has been altered by 'third parties,' blocs, bolts and other variations. The almost immediate adoption by the National Assembly of a rough organization according to groups, and the subsequent recurrence of this method in most countries under parliamentary rule, certainly suggest that

the group system is at least a viable one. It may well be argued that if the main function of a parliament is not to govern, but to provide a focus for public opinion for the guidance of the governors, then *the group system, since it frankly accepts existing diversity of opinion, is better than a two-party system which tries to gloss over such a diversity.*

2.66 In Light of Modern Political History, the Christian Task

This should give us Christians courage to introduce such discussions into the political life of our countries. Of course, such opinions of our contemporaries are not the source of the courage we must display. That is the Word of God. We are not only called to be witnesses of the Truth; we are also "begotten with the word of truth, that we should be a kind of firstfruits of his creatures" (James 1:18). We should be first with a political message based on *realities* revealed in the Word. That is our reforming task in the world for which we are qualified by the Spirit of God, Who applies the Word of God to our hearts at the beginning of our "way," and thus renews the problematics of our "walk" from the beginning. In this work we can derive much profit from the labours of Abraham Kuyper and the Dutch Anti-revolutionary Party.

Having seen in what way the Word of God directs our political "goings" from the beginning, and what the nature of the present political world really is, we shall have to, I believe, come to the conclusion, that there is only one course for us to take: the building of a community of opinion and the forming of a Christian political party as an instrument for the accomplishing of the necessary integral reformation of our political life. The forming of such a party will itself bring an important reorganization and realignment in Canadian society, the strongest kind of witnessing in the biblical sense of the word.

Lecture III:
SYNTHESIS

3.0 Its Contemporary Political Expression

[It has become clear that neither time nor space will permit me to develop my third lecture in the way I had originally planned. Let us hope that sometime in the future the opportunity will present itself to treat this material in a way commensurate with its historical significance, with the degree of devastation it has wrought in our personal lives, with its effective weakening of the cultural struggle in which we are called to engage, with its sapping of the spiritual energies with which the people of God are to witness to the Truth in the midst of the world. For the moment I shall attempt in very brief compass to touch on the most important points I had wished to discuss.]

3.1 Summary of Preceding

WE HAVE SEEN THAT CHRISTIAN political action in the scriptural sense – remember the general title of these lectures – is very far from being the support of this or that particular measure, and is certainly not the supporting of particular issues because they are (thought to be) in the interest of instituted churches or of blocs of Christian citizens (who have certain social and economic "rights" to be guarded) or of a public morality deemed by some church or other to be desirable; but that it is an articulation for the political aspect of our life of the integral Gospel of Jesus Christ, that it is a battle for a political order that is in conformity with the divine Order of Creation (sphere-sovereignty), that it is an effort at fundamental and integral reformation or renewal of our political life from out of the Word of God, the Principium of our whole life and the Republication of the divine Thesis (see Lecture I). If, then, in addition, the various organizations of political effort in our modern world are shown to be, in one way or another and in a manner more or less confident, consistent and intense, articulations of an opposing or antithetical (pseudo-principle of Order, of freedom, of authority; and if sometimes, in addition, the *total organization* of the forms of political effort within a particular national territory is intended to express the choice of political directions that is possible or tolerable within a supposed community of reason, so that the political alternatives must be complementary rather than antagonistic to each other, this form of total organization thus witnessing to the oneness of the race and the possibility of community outside of an obedient submission to the life-sustaining Law of God and in this way failing to present to men *the real*, the basically meaningful choice there is in our human life between all those ways that are in principle disobedient (since they "construct" another principle) and ways obedient to the Law of God as revealed in His Word (Lecture II); then it is not adequate, indeed it is not possible, for a Christian who wishes to perform his political duty to God to enter one or another of these organizations of conviction and effort to which men in the grip of modern ideas (or at best in the grip of watered down Christianity or a syncretistic religious attitude accommodated to modern humanist ideas) have given form (as the *expression* of their idea), and to try to exercise a "Christian" influence in it. For "Christian" *in the scriptural sense* requires a fundamental and integral (*whole* as *one*) attack on the very idea that gives the modern organization its meaning and its long-range direction and influence.

Nor can the Christian, whose life is to be integrally directed by Scripture, decide on a policy of flitting from one of these modern organizations to another. For the salvation the Word of God brings, also for the political aspect of our lives, is not to be found by an attempted balancing, for example, of the "order" and "security" of socialism with the "freedom" of liberalism. "Order" and "security" and "authority" and "freedom" are understood in the light of the Gospel, and they do not have the same meanings in the movements we know as conservatism, liberalism, socialism and communism. A wrong idea of freedom (as in liberalism) – which is also enslaving and destructive, because only the new life in Christ brings a salutary issue in our human walk – cannot be made to "balance out" a wrong idea of authority (as in conservatism). The Word of God must take *integral* hold on us, so that our view of all these matters will be *reformed according to the Truth*. Our political witness must be of this radical and integral kind. If it is not, it neither illumines the darkened situation nor brings ways of salvation in our "goings."

3.2 Necessity and Fruitfulness of Organization

If we are to get beyond the field of influence of the revolutionary ideas and clearly articulate the Principle of God's Word over against the pseudo-principle which modern forms of political effort articulate in one way or another; if over against the falling away (apostasy) from Meaning of liberalism and conservatism, of socialism and communism, we are to declare, as faithful servants of Jesus Christ and ambassadors of His reconciliation, the Truth of God, then we shall have to *organize our integral Christian conviction*. When we do so we shall bring such a witness that, with God's blessing, a *realignment of political forces* will really come about in the national life. Just as the erection of the Free Reformed University of Amsterdam compelled unwilling humanists to "recognize," in a certain practical way, the reality of a basic religious difference in the life of mankind that is significant for the way men go in the world of studies, and just as the work of the A.R.S.S. will force men to face up to the problems and issues they would otherwise not have to decide because modern organizations gloss over and conceal the most real difference there is among men, so also the organization of an integrally Christian political effort will press upon our fellow men the *reality* that a religious Principle directs our whole life and that there is a deep religious dividedness in our race. This need not lead to Wars of Religion, as we have seen, but could bring a peaceable living with one another in the light of *realities*, a peaceable seeking of political ways of living together that *recognize* the hard reality of the root-character of religion and the root-dividedness of our race within the Order of Creation.

This itself is certainly a highly desirable objective. There is no Christian witness, in the scriptural sense of "Christian," in attempting to live constantly with humanistically devised forms of political life which darken men's understanding of *reality*, thereby of necessity neglecting the prophetic-priestly-kingly Office of man in Christ to *reform* these forms in order to bring our life more into conformity with the demands of the salutary Law of God and thus see His salvation incorporated in the national life of our people.

3.3 Simple Evangelical Obedience

Finally then, by such political organization as we have suggested we not only witness to the reality of the Antithesis; we not only offer a *genuine political choice* that derives its *meaningfulness* from the fact that it accords with the real lines of division that lie at the very heart of the dynamic unfolding of our human life and thus expresses – I almost want to say existentially (not existentialistically) – the meaning of the religious history of mankind, in this way too making the best possible contribution to getting out of our present political doldrums (for we have seen that the apathy and seemingly meaningless drift in today's political "life" is to be ascribed to a loss of belief in a guiding principle and the absence of any really meaningful choice between existing organizations of political effort – here Mr. Knowles sees well, although he chooses, as is understandable for a modern man, a more radical articulation of the pseudo-principle and thus does not provide the solution of a genuine choice between directing principles); but *we are simply doing the plain task that the Word of God lays upon us as Christians.*

3.4 The Present Situation

How then, if this can so categorically be stated, does it come that we find no such integrally Christian political witness anywhere around us on this North American continent? How is it that instead, what we do find, is the very sort of thing we have repeatedly been rejecting throughout these lectures?

a. Mass Man

For it is a fact that many confessors of the name of Christ appear to differ little from the typical "mass man" of the twentieth century, who simply accepts whatever cultural forms he finds in his immediate surroundings and makes daily use of them without any recognition of the human effort that was involved in first giving them form and then handing them down, also without thanksgiving, without any sense of responsibility – the modern loss of the sense of man as man-in-Office! – for preserving and constantly reforming them in the light of the Norm. How is this possible? For we saw in the first lecture that the political task is an integral part of the Calling of the Christian, and cannot be left to "experts."

b. Conservatism

Moreover, many Protestant Christians who have done some thinking about politics have been and often still are attached in one way or another to the conservative movement. In Canada, for instance, the Conservative Party traditionally consisted largely of the established English ruling classes, the theologically Calvinist Scotch Presbyterians and those descendants of America's Pilgrim Fathers who had come up to Canada. How is this possible? For I explained in my second lecture that, although, historically, conservatism was an effort to combat the progressivist principle of the Revolution, it was as such a complete failure because it stopped short of living out of the Light of the only genuine Principle of life which can overcome the revolutionary pseudo-principle, the life-bestowing and life-directing Word of the living God, and it perverted the true nature of Office by pulling it down from its religious place and meaning and identifying it with historically established interests and rights, thereby depriving itself of any Criterion by which it could judge between that in the historical unfolding of our life which is good (according to the Norm), and thus should be conserved, and that which is evil, and thus should be reformed (again by the dynamic and reformatorical cultural labours of men in accordance with the Norm). As an effort at providing different *direction* in political life conservatism has completely petered out; it has become effete. The efforts of a Russell Kirk will be unavailing unless he, like Groen van Prinsterer, gets beyond conservatism to a political articulation of the divine Thesis as republished in the Gospel. Where so many Christians attach themselves to conservatism the power of the Gospel in them is rendered politically saltless. How can such things be?

c. More Dynamic Movements

In this light it is understandable that many of the younger generation of Christians, wishing to be more dynamic, are seen to be engaged in making the change-over to more liberal movements. In Europe and in certain "broader" American Protestant circles, increasing numbers of men who call themselves Christian have even turned to exploring what they call a "Christian socialism." In our own "more conservative" circles we have scarcely got farther than liberalism, but in our immediate church circles we have the unsavoury situation that the political effort and the votes of one "half" of us are cancelling out the political influence of the other "half." This is even defended by saying that "we" must make our influence felt *everywhere*. A colleague of mine to whom I spoke about this matter after our last presidential campaign passed off the curious remark that after the election he feels like taking some aspirin and sleeping it off. Could this be the beginning of a realization that something has gone wrong? It scarcely sounds like the MAN of God, by the Word and Spirit of God thoroughly furnished unto every good work, working in confident faith towards the Consummation of our salvation at the Last Day! What, again, is the meaning of all this?

d. Preoccupation with Immediacies

Everywhere we find Christians in politics scurrying around, just as our western politicians in general are doing, dealing one by one with detail-questions, immediate problems they bump up against, suddenly exploding crises, without any understanding of the principles that have been operative in the bringing about of these "factual" situations, and even without any understanding, in the circumstances, of the guiding light of their life's Principle. These men are constantly hearing "conservative" attitudes expressed, and "liberal" ones, perhaps even socialistic ones, and they attempt to find a resolution of their difficulty in terms of these "immediacies," oblivious to the clash of principle that is, under present organization of our political life, greatly obscured, thus allowing us all constantly to be drawn to the Left. Many Christians in politics even speak scornfully of all talk about principles being operative in *factual* political situations, and show how caught up they are in the immediate modern situation and the modern mentality (and thus how *little* they are directed from out of the Word) by repeating the empty propaganda of our time, – e.g., to quote a sample I picked up in my immediate Christian environment not very long ago, that "Romney might very well be good presidential material if we happen to be in a depression at the time we need a candidate." Brethren, how can these things be?

e. Christian "Class War"

We can even find in our own Christian circles the "class war" in faint miniature, as when one member of our churches who has managed to climb up the economic ladder to a solid automobile dealership informs me that he votes Republican because he is thus assured of protection of his interests – and that he be so well cared for is certainly good for the churches, isn't it, since the church surely needs a lot of money?! –, while, a few days later, another member of the same church informs me that he always votes Democrat because that is the party which remembers the common people – here he comes with some vague reference to the "*kleine luyden*" (little people) of Abraham Kuyper. (Now I am sure that all of us "common people" ought to be "remembered," but is this the criterion of a Christian political effort? Are the "little people" "remembered" in the Democratic Party *in the right way*? Is there but one people, reduced to the big economic "haves" and the little economic "have-nots"? Or is there a religiously split humanity, the life of which is much more complex and deep than its social-economic functions? Are the "common people" of this man's Democratic Party the same as Abraham Kuyper's *kleine luyden*, and is the "remembering" the same in both instances? Is not rationalism's reductionist view of society at work here, *but unobserved by the Christian* who identifies himself with the political strivings of this party?)

Nevertheless, in this way Christians themselves make an opening for the standpoint that the history of mankind is dominated by the economic class war, the heart of which is the notion of the coercion of the "have-nots" by the "haves," which grew up in the course of the Industrial Revolution in the West and belongs to the capitalist phase of economic development in an expanding industrialism. Here the polarity of conservative and liberal was absorbed into the idea of the class war. How now does it come that we can hear such things among Christians?

3.5 Christian Political Action Is Lacking

Everywhere we look we neither hear nor see anything of a people of God, an Order of Creation, the Office of man restored in Christ, but only find our Christian people scattered in all camps making use of the usual tools of the trade: they recommend lobbies and pressure groups to safeguard and promote the interests of "our people"; they spearhead citizens' actions to ensure "good government" (which, incidentally, means something which unbelievers caught up in the modern revolutionary mentality can perfectly agree with) and a "public morality" congenial to respectable middle-class citizens. What, indeed, is the meaning of all this?

3.6 Individuality of Judgment Not the Explanation

One thing is certain: it may not be explained – though efforts are often made in this direction – by appealing to the *individuality* and *relativity* of our judgment in a *baffling diversity* of circumstances. Such individualism, we have seen, is untrue to reality. Behind all the diversity of circumstances and the manifold of facts *religious principle* is operative. Likewise, our judgment in its religious depth-level is directed by the one Word of

God or by an "imagined" substitute. Life as a whole, life in its entirety, is religion. As God's creation, the world, including all the cultural activity of believers and unbelievers alike, is *an order of law*. Even the lawlessness of men is bound by the Law of God. Into our fallen life a WORD has come from God, a living and powerful Principle which begets us to new life and directs all its "goings." The Word of God establishes a *COMMUNITY in the Truth*.

No; Christians are not severally abandoned to their *individual* judgments in a multitude of individual situations. As a matter of fact, *this very attempt* on the part of Christians *to explain the differences of opinion* that are to be found among them when it comes to judging our cultural, specifically now, our political, responsibility *by means of an individualistic theory* points to the deeper cause: the synthesis mind. (After all, to employ an individualistic theory when the Word of God precludes such is at one point *not* to be directed by the Word of God!)

3.7 The Explanation Is the Synthesis Mind

No; not some unaccountable and seemingly irresolvable difference of judgment among Christians with which somehow we shall simply have to learn to live – which would mean that there is no common Word of God to be a Light for our path –, but a failure on the part of Christians to give the Word of God the place in their lives *that it demands for itself*, a failure to sense the true nature of the divine Word or the role it (sovereignly!) comes to fulfill as radical directing Principium of our whole life in its integral unity, – this is the cause of our present differences with respect to our cultural task and the means by which we are to accomplish it. This will repeatedly be denied; it is true nevertheless. It is not that we judge historical situations differently; it is, when you come right down to it, that in judging historical situations we make a different use of the Word of God. The present differences about our political task among Reformed Christians on this continent stem, in the first place, *from different attitudes towards the Word of God itself,* towards the role it has to play in directing our judgment about those historical situations; stem, basically, from different positions as to the *range of the Word's validity.*

3.8 Contemporary Illustrations of the Synthesis Mind

To demonstrate that such is the case permit me to refer to a couple of articles dealing with our subject that have appeared in recent years in Christian Reformed circles in the United States. Before citing these articles there is something of a personal nature on my heart that I must say to you. In the past I have had experiences which indicate that there is a certain danger involved in publicly criticizing articles that have been written by men in whose close proximity we do our daily work. It has greatly surprised me to find that such criticism is here and there looked upon as something closely akin to a hostile act. In all sincerity I want to ask, Is this not a childish and foolish attitude? How could scientific investigations and the so very necessary polemic or clash of views ever be conducted in such a stifling atmosphere? Are the published articles not attempts to get at the truth of the matter? Are these articles above criticism? Is the truth or our personal prestige paramount? If there is not yet agreement among us on subjects that are publicly discussed, may the existing disagreement not be expressed? Is not the important thing that all of us together, as the people of God, come to a fuller and fuller acknowledgement of the authority of the Word of God over our lives? To that end, is not a constantly advancing discussion about the principles that govern our life-expression (thought and acts) healthy and even highly necessary? I should not have to say, among Christians, that in my criticism of these articles there is nothing of personal rancor, that no effort is here being made to establish my authority above the authority of another. In my criticism there is only a determined effort, in the light of the Word of God, to understand the relation of that Word to our life-in-the-world; it is a debate on the level of *principial reflection.*

Furthermore, obviously I am not claiming that the present opinions of the writers whose articles I am going to cite are identical with the opinions they expressed in their articles. I am dealing with published expressions of opinion, which, as such, were evidently intended to influence other men's opinions, and I am – that must also be said – unaware of any efforts having been made to withdraw or to modify these opinions. As far as is known, they stand there still as efforts to influence the mind of the Christian body, and as such I shall deal with them.

3.9 The First Article

The first article, "A Look at the Dutch" by Dr. John T. Daling, appeared in *The Reformed Journal*, Vol. vii, No. 5 (May, 1957), pp. 22-27. While much in this article calls for comment, at present there is only time to make one rather central criticism. You will remember that I am using this and one other article as examples of the fact that our different attitudes towards, for example, the organizing of a radical and integral Christian political activity stem, not from a relativity of judgment in complex historical situations which somehow proves irreducible, but essentially from different fundamental attitudes – demonstrably there, whether intended or not – as to the relation of the Word of God to our life-in-the-world, from different views as to the range of validity of the Word of God.

On p. 25 (col. 1, par. 5) Prof. Daling, speaking of the division of Dutch political and social life "along philosophico-religious (or confessional) lines," uses the word "tripartitism," which means (divided into) three parts – this itself is not correct: besides the liberal, Protestant and Roman Catholic movements he mentions there is the very important socialist movement of the Labour Party (Partij van de Arbeid) and the recently organized P.S.P. (Pacifistisch Socialistische Partij), – and says:

> I am quite sure that the cause for this "tripartitism" is not directly a "principial" deduction from a specific theological system. Rather, tripartitism has general historical origins and has been conditioned or influenced sociologically. Its roots are embedded deep in past ages of tradition, and of social as well as religious conflict.

3.10 Analysis of First Article

What I want you to notice in this statement is, first, that our living according to the Word of God is not understood as RELIGION in the sense in which we have come to see that in these Unionville Conferences, but as "'principial' deduction from a theological system." The Christian religion has been narrowed down – scientistically – to a theological system; this system of thought, and not the Word of God as a living and powerful integral Word that takes hold of our hearts, illumines us and directs all our "goings" in history and society, is viewed as the "principle"; and from this theological system of thought "'principial' deductions" for life can be made. *But that life is there.* In the second place, therefore, observe that over against that "world" of "'principial' deduction from a specific theological system" a second "world" is posited of historical development and sociological influence. After a typical scientistic reduction of the Christian religion to theology and possible "deductions" from such a theological system for life, a great world of history and society is left over *which somehow independently of theology* (religion understood in that sense) *also directs our "goings."* That this analysis of ours is correct, and that the most serious consequences are involved, can be seen from a basic section of the article (on p. 27, col. 1), where we read:

> I have now become convinced that the Dutch way is part of the Dutch system; that the Dutch system is a highly integrated, very involved, and delicately balanced system; that this system has been greatly conditioned both historically and sociologically; and that many of the Reformed 'positions' and 'practices' in the cultural areas are, almost inevitably, more a result of historical and sociological conditioning than of 'principial' considerations. Consequently, to incorporate without significant qualifications a part of the Dutch system, whether from the social, economic, political, educational, or ecclesiastical area – even on the ground of 'Reformedness' – into another system (be it American, South African, Hungarian, North African, Ceylonese, Japanese, etc.) is, at the very least, to have an unintelligent disregard for history and sociology. The Dutch way, including 'Reformedness' in cultural areas, work (sic!) out fairly well for the Dutch because they are

Dutch, that is, because their whole historical and sociological complex is peculiar to them.

It is folly to argue whether the Dutch system is better than the American or the American better than the Dutch. That would be like arguing whether a pear is better than a peach. Both systems or ways can be described and analyzed with respect to various features and characteristics, but to compare them as to betterness is futile. They are simply different. No doubt the Dutch way is better than the American way for the Dutch, but from this it does not follow that the Dutch system is better for the Americans. Both systems have had different historical roots and sociological conditioning. If we really believe that God reveals Himself in history, then the fact of cultural difference must be taken seriously.

In the words "more a result of historical and sociological conditioning than of 'principial' considerations" we encounter the typically scholastic *limitation* of the range of validity of the revealed truths of faith (the Word of God viewed as the source of a theological system), *and the consequent emergence of great areas of life that are conceived as over against, thus outside, the sphere of influence of our theological (!) principle,* the scholastic "world" of nature (and history). Prof. Daling is so sure of the independence from religion (to him, theology with deductions) of what he calls historical and sociological (he must be using "sociological" in the sense of "social") influences that he declares that the "Dutch way, *including 'Reformedness' in cultural areas, work* (sic!) out fairly well for the Dutch because they are Dutch, that is, because their whole historical and sociological complex is peculiar to them" [italics mine – H.E.R.].

Prof. Daling thus sees the cultural "ways" of the Dutch as

governed rather by this "historical and sociological complex" which is peculiarly Dutch than by religious principle, and what, in the light of his whole argument, he is really saying is that what men often grow accustomed to calling "Reformed" in cultural activity is not that at all, but simply the historical development of peculiar conditions of Dutch society, and that to go on thinking of such cultural activities as directed by a *religious* (theological) principle is only to go on deceiving oneself.

Mind you, I am not at this point taking up the cudgels for the specific program of any actual Christian organization in the Netherlands or anywhere else, as though some particular program or other is indeed "Reformed." What interests me here in Prof. Daling's analysis is that he argues that such cultural activity is not really 'Reformed' so much as *historically* or *sociologically* influenced. It is this putting of history and society *over against* "Reformed" that says so much. Prof. Daling might, for instance, have said that if such an organizational activity is not really "Reformed" (i.e., for him, directed essentially by a "principial" deduction from a "Reformed" theological system), it is then conservative, or liberal, or Marxist, or whatever. But he does not – and this I find highly significant – put one faith over against another. Over against a (scholastically reduced and scientifically conceived) Reformed "principle" he puts historical and sociological influences, which, now, he views as independent of the direction of a religious "principle."

First, then, there is his failure to see the Word of God as directive for all our "ways" ("ways" that have "made" our history and given form to our society), and to see that *all* of life is thus (integrally) religion, either true or apostate. Second, he sets up other "aspects" of life, viz. historical and sociological, and gives them a real *autonomy* with respect to his religious (reduced theological) principle.

3.11 Supposed Extra-Religious Direction of Life

What, actually, is this "historical and sociological complex"? It is independent, concrete life, – but, cut off from (the direction of) religion (theology). It is the scholastic's "world" of "Nature," and it too (that is, besides religion, in Prof. Daling's scientistic-reductionist understanding of it, which, by means of deductions from a theological system directs *some* of our "goings," viz. the "principial" ones) is directive of our cultural "ways."

3.12 Culture as an Organism

How is it thus directive? Here Prof. Daling resorts to the analogy of an organism. A culture, say Dutch or American culture, is like an organism. The "ways" of a culture that develop are like the developing characteristics of an organism. Just as the skin and taste of a peach develop from the inner nature or "peachness" of the peach, the peculiar and unique peach-nature, so the "ways" of a culture are the outgrowth or expression of the unique nature of the cultural life-system in the midst of which they arise. The "ways" are "directed" by the inner nature of the culture. Viewed in this light, the "ways" of cultures can never be "argued" as better or worse: each culture gives rise (necessarily) to ways that are "proper" to it. The "ways" of one culture when introduced into another would be only dangerous "*fremde Korper.*"

"Cultural transplants" are impossible, generally. In this way

Prof. Daling can conclude that

> it is folly to argue whether the Dutch system is better than the American or the American better than the Dutch. *That would be like arguing whether a pear is better than a peach* – [italics mine – H.E.R.]. Both systems or ways can be described and analyzed with respect to various features and characteristics, but to compare them as to betterness is futile. They are simply *different*.

Prof. Daling proceeds to draw the very dangerous conclusion: "If we really believe that God reveals Himself in history, then the fact of cultural difference must be taken seriously." This is the absolutizing of what has historically developed, seen apart from the one divine Norm. How does Prof. Daling get out of this cultural and historical relativism?

3.13 Anti-Scriptural View of Culture

We are familiar with the view that cultures are like organisms from the work of men like Spengler and Toynbee. *It is one viewpoint about human culture, but not a scripturally directed viewpoint.* The development of human society is not like the ripening (and rotting) of a pear. Man heads the creation in the (religious) position of Office, and the "ways" he finds to live his life he finds in the (religious) Ways of obedience or of disobedience to the divine Law, including many kinds of *norm-law*, which are laws of another kind than the natural laws according to which peaches and pears ripen. It is not true that we cannot compare the "ways" of cultures as to better or worse: there is one God and divine Law above us all, and mankind is a religious community, directed by the Word of God or an imagined distorting substitute.

The fact is that it is not possible to hold a scripturally directed view of human society (such as can be seen, in outline, in our Groen Club syllabus, *The Bible and the Life of the Christian*, see esp. the chapters on Culture and on Human Society) and this (apostate) organismic view. Prof. Daling can do it only because he has already reduced the scriptural revelation about religion and principle. His "mind" is a synthesis-mind, a *divided* (not integral) mind.

3.14 A Second Contemporary Expression of Synthesis

It is exceedingly important to see the point I am here making if we are to come to a scripturally directed integral Christian life on this North American continent. For we are surrounded by deeply entrenched ways of thinking which only such a synthesis-mind makes "possible." For example, we find the same organismic view of culture expressed in the second article to which I want to call attention in the present discussion, the article "Calvinism and Political Action" by Dr. William Spoelhof. This article has frequently been recommended for study. We should give it our close attention. It is found in the volume *God-Centered Living*, a symposium published by the (American) Calvinistic Action Committee in 1951, pp. 159-173. Again, there is much in the article that calls for comment, but I must now confine myself to this organismic view of culture which also underlies Dr. Spoelhof's thinking. Let me quote a few sentences bearing on the point.

> There are several propositions, basic to all types of political action in America, which must be understood thoroughly before any one type of action can be contemplated. The first, and most important

of these, is: political institutions, just as social, economic, and cultural institutions are outgrowths or expressions of a national consciousness. Political institutions, no matter where they are found, express the genius of the nation in which they develop. As such, these institutions are never mere transplantations developed successfully elsewhere… French institutions are what they are because they are French, and Dutch institutions are Dutch, and American institutions are American… Political institutions and political action within the forms and structures of any particular country must grow out of the "*volkskarakter*" and be adjusted to their own native distinctiveness… We must work within the sphere of American political tradition and practice and not attempt to impose methods and approaches which are novel to the American scene… A confessional political party would run counter to the whole American tradition and, as such, would not be palatable to any great number of Americans, not even among many who style themselves Calvinists… American political parties are by and large based on men and on expediency and not on principles… European parties seek to *divide* men into cohesive political groups on the basis of principles and ideologies. The American political parties, on the other hand, do not *divide* but *unite* men of conflicting and contrary principles and ideologies… The party programs must therefore of necessity be general, because no party can afford to affront a large block of interests if it wishes to win an election. Fixed dogma, rigid adherence to a body of principles, and a consistently-adhered-to permanent program are foreign therefore to our party system.

3.15 Alarming Conclusions of These Articles

And then this much of Dr. Spoelhof's conclusion:

From this brief presentation of the nature of the American party system a series of conclusions affecting Calvinistic political action in America can be drawn... In the first place, any attempt to form an effective political party on the basis of uncompromising principles is doomed to failure. This holds true whatever those principles may be, but it is doubly true if those principles are confessional in nature.

It would seem to me that if we are to live by the Principle of the Word of God then what Dr. Spoelhof is saying is that any attempt to live consistently by that Word is doomed to failure in America. That Word, however, has this remarkable POW-ER, that it begets to new life. And it must be proclaimed. And it promises great blessing to obedience. Therefore I am greatly alarmed when I read, as the conclusion also of Prof. Daling's article, that

> our task is to live out the Reformed *faith* in an American way in the American system. This system has roots, conditions, and a genius which are quite different from those of the Dutch... But now it is time... for us Americans to set forth the Reformed *faith* in terms of our own genius.

If our "system" and our "genius" are not religion-directed, what are they then? Whence their existence, their direction? What is there that exists free from the creation-situation and the direction of the Law of God?

3.16 Synthesis the Culprit

In these two articles we meet all the familiar terms of this *world-ly* outlook – I use the adjective advisedly to mean an outlook which, ignoring the fundamental religious relation of the entire creation to the Creator, attempts to understand the *world in terms of itself* – on human culture: *Volksgeist, volkskarakter,* genius. It is a view that became prominent in the so-called Historical Right School of jurisprudence in the middle of the nineteenth century, and, as we have seen, became part of the arsenal of the conservative movement. Office and authority were, we saw, brought down from their religious meaning to become attached to what has historically grown. Culture is seen as something enclosed within itself, like the development of a fruit to maturation, not as a religious life before the face of the living God in terms of His Law-order. Just think, if we should take this theory seriously, then all those gigantic struggles of faith by which the Dutch Christians of a century ago fought for Lebensraum against the oppressive liberalism which then had a stranglehold on Dutch culture would turn out to be nothing more than the natural expression of the Dutch genius! We are compelled to ask ourselves: How is it possible that among men who are Christians views can continue to be held that are not only in conflict with the integral Light of the Word of God but are also such clear distortions of what God has accomplished in the midst of an obedient people? The answer is: SYNTHESIS.

3.17 What Synthesis Is

What, now, is this synthesis, really? Synthesis is a long and powerful destructive tradition in Christian circles. It is not the same as eclecticism, which usually means that a selection of limited or *detail* insights is brought together from a variety of sources without regard to the systematic principles which in the original sources gave these details their specific meaning. Synthesis has just exactly to do with principles of total-structuration. In our several Unionville Conferences we have seen that the Truth is one, that the Word of God is the integral Principle of our life in that it is a Re-publication of the integral religious sense of the creation-order, and that rebellious men religiously "imagine" pseudo-principles of *total*-structuration, which, deprived of the Light of Truth, vitiate the meaning of the *whole*. Synthesis is the attempt to hold together the Truth of the Word of God *and* someone or other of these apostate constructions of the *total*-meaning of existence. I have discussed it in my third lecture of our first Conference (see *Christian Perspectives*, 1960, p. 140f.) and in both my lectures last year (*Christian Perspectives*, 1961). Of course, since the Word of God and the efforts of Greek philosophical thought are both statements about the totality of meaning, and the latter are a religious apostasy or falling away from the meaning of God's Truth proclaimed in the former, the effort to hold them together can never really be successful.

3.18 Its Impossibility

Barrett has seen something of this (*Irrational Man*, p. 82):

> St. Paul locates this center in faith, Aristotle in reason; and these two conceptions, worlds apart, show how at its very fountainhead the Christian understanding of man diverges utterly from that of Greek philosophy, *however much later thinkers may have tried to straddle this gulf* [italics mine – H.E.R.].

The same writer, just a little farther on (idem, p. 88) again shows remarkable insight when he says:

The medieval harmony was achieved at a price: In the thought of St. Thomas Aquinas…, the crowning work of the synthesis, man is – to use Bernard Groethuysen's image – really a centaur, a being divided between the natural and theological orders. In the natural order Thomistic man is Aristotelian – a creature whose center is reason and whose substantial form is the rational soul; and St. Thomas, the Christian, never bats an eye in commenting upon the passage in Aristotle's *Ethics* which states flatly that reason is our true and real self, the center of our personal identity, but merely expounds it in straightforward agreement. This might be excused as simply the pedagogic exposition of a teacher identifying himself with his text; but in the *Summa Theologica* he repeats that the speculative, or theoretical, intellect is the highest function of man, that to which all the others are subordinate. This rational animal in the natural order is subordinated, to be sure, to the supernatural; but again through an intellectual vision – the final one, of the essence of God – which informs and purifies the will. This is a synthesis indeed, but how far we have traveled from the experience of Biblical man or of the early Christian, whose faith was felt as something that pierced the bowels and the belly of a man's spirit!

3.19 Synthesis Has a Long History

Yes; such synthesis is indeed in principle impossible. And yet, throughout the long centuries of the Church's history it has been a dominant characteristic of the thinking of Christians. At first, the so-called church fathers, reared in either one or other Greek philosophical system before being converted to Christianity, came later – consciously or unconsciously – to *read the Scriptures in the light of those Greek systems*. The content of the Scripture, or *theologia*, was thought of as the *philosophia Christiana*, or Christian counterpart of Greek philosophy, but a whole world of pagan thought, which in reality, being devoid of a knowledge of the Truth, was a repressing religious substitute for that Truth, had in this way been introduced into the thinking of Christians, and sanctioned with scriptural authority. (Prof. Vollenhoven calls this the method of eisegesis and exegesis, i.e., of reading in and then reading out.) A prominent example is the Greek intellectualist view of "natural law," which was read into the scriptural revelation of the Truth at such places as Romans, chapters 1 and 2. (To get some insight into this gigantic confusion of two worlds of thought, compare the discussion in the first nine chapters of Carlyle and Carlyle, *A History of Medieval Political Theory in the West* with chapters seven and eight of Berkouwer, *De Algemene Openbaring* – English, *General Revelation* – which deal with the first two chapters of Romans.)

In this *patristic synthesis* a sifting of the products of (apostate-religiously directed) Greek philosophical reflection from the true meaning of God's revelation was needed. *Such* a sifting, unfortunately, did not come, but in the *scholastic synthesis* a separation of the Greek philosophical material (including a rational or "natural" theology) was made from the material of christian or revealed theology. In this fashion also men distinguished between philosophy and (christian) theology. Now the results of the Greek philosophical tradition were recognized for what they were and *were allowed to stand* as a certain 'natural' preamble to christian (i.e. scripture-directed) theology. *Here for the first time in Christian circles traditional Greek philosophical thought (including that rational or natural theology) was declared principially free from the direction of revealed or supranatural the-ology (i.e. scripture, though understood scientistically).*

3.20 Synthesis in American Puritanism

This scholastic synthesis is to be seen, for example, in a man who was one of the chief "authorities" of the Puritans who came to America, Johann Heinrich Alsted of Herborn (1588-1638), when he divides theology into *theologia naturalis* and *theologia supranaturalis.* The former is for him that theology *"quae procedit e principiis naturali intellectus lumine notis, pro rationis humanae modo,"* while *theologia supranaturalis alias arcana,* on the other hand, provides a knowledge *"quae procedit e principiis notis lumine fidei, supra (at non praeter, non contra) humanae rationis modum."*

Protestant scholasticism from the beginning found a home among the American Puritans; such scholastic thought distinguished a truth reached by the "natural" reason from the truth communicated by revelation and appropriated by faith. The integral-religious nature of man (which does not allow for an independently functioning "natural" reason) and of the Truth was lost sight of. Since the realm of "Nature" was actually the *anti*-scriptural thought-results of Greek philosophy, an increasing tension arose between the two so-called "worlds" of "Nature" and of "Grace." In later scholastics the two "truths" diverged to the point of being in disagreement and yet both "true." For the scholastic motif continued to be held, in the words, again, of our Protestant scholastic, Alsted: *"Gratia non destruit naturam, sed earn perfecit... Natura gratiam commendat, gratia naturam emendat"* (i.e. theological Lehnsatze, "principial" deductions from a theological system which are *a kind of marginal correction*, but no integral reformation, of a life that possesses its own laws of development).

3.21 And in American Calvinism

This Protestant scholasticism dominated, in the late nineteenth century, in the very citadel of orthodox Presbyterianism in the States. Prof. A.A. Hodge, of the famous family of Princeton Seminary theologians, in his *Outlines of Theology* (ed. 1863, p. 49f.) wrote: "We define reason to be man's natural faculty of reaching the truth, including his understanding, heart, conscience and experience, acting under natural circumstances, and without any supernatural assistance. And we define faith, on the other hand, to be the assent of the mind" — please note! — "to truth, upon the testimony of God, conveying knowledge to us through supernatural channels . . . Reason establishes the fact that God speaks, but when we know what He says, we believe it because He says it." (Compare also what I wrote in *Christian Perspectives*, 1960, p. 154f., and further, Richard R. Niebuhr, *Resurrection and Historical Reason*, e.g. pp. 105-125).

3.22 Consequence: Powerlessness of Christians

Where such an *independent* world of nature and of reason was accepted, independent in principle from the religious direction (and thus also reformation) of the Word of God, there Christians could, besides holding to their traditionally received theology (with its "principial" deductions for life, or Lehnsatze), follow along with the current modes of thought that appealed to the "reason" of their time and situation. The Christian religion having been restricted to a *supra-natural* realm of revealed theology, the Christian as *homo rationalis* was *free* (from Scripture) to adopt whatever men generally found "reasonable" for this life of nature, of history, of natural society. Christians who have followed the synthetic pattern have generally followed along in the development of modern man's "mind," from his acceptance of an absolute *a priori* "principle," to the relativizing of this *a priori*, to the confession that we are "guided" only by the positive "facts," to the present pragmatic-opportunism. All idea of "bringing all things back to a right relation to the Father," all idea of reformational activity in cultural areas, disappeared. This "*mitmenschliche*" deterioration, this solidarity with our fellow man along his lost "way," was modified only by a dry-as-dust and even deadly repetition of traditional theological formulations, out of which all full-orbed reformatorical power was gone. Because POWER is in the Word of God as Principle of our integral life. Here we witness the present powerlessness of the Christian Body in this most fundamental crisis of our culture.

3.23 Our Hope and Our STRENGTH

It is this Protestant scholasticism, this synthesis-"mind," that accounts for present views among us about Christian cultural activity. Our hope is that through our Unionville Conferences and through the witness of the A.R.S.S. the desire will grow among all of us Christians to join whole-heartedly in the psalmist's prayer: Integrate my heart in the fear of Thy Name. We must learn anew that we are the People of the Principle of life. We need not fear. The whole revelation of God in His Word is full of illustrations that man must be weak in order for God to reveal His strength. The power to renew the life of mankind is in the Word of the living God. We are only to witness to that Word, and we will see the WONDER of God's power.

I should like to end these lectures with a quotation from Prof. H. Dooyeweerd, *A New Critique of Theoretical Thought*, II 364f.:

> (The Christian Idea of cultural development) continues to observe the inner tension between sinful reality and the full demand of the Divine Law... This demand is terrifying when we consider how much the temporal ordinances labour under the destructive power of the fall into sin. Terrifying also, when it puts before us our task as Christians in the struggle for the power of cultural formation. For it makes a demand on us which as sinful human beings we cannot satisfy in any way. And it urges us, in the misery of our hearts, to seek refuge with Christ, from Whose fullness, nevertheless, a Christian can derive the confidence of faith to carry on the ceaseless struggle for the control of 'cultural' development. This is the remarkable 'nevertheless' of Christian faith... Christian philosophic thought has to fight shy of self-exaltation, because it is directed in its root to Christ. The whole struggle that positive Christianity has to carry on for the direction of the opening-process is not directed against our fellow-men, in whose sin we partake and whose guilt is ours and whom we should love as our neighbours. That struggle is directed against the spirit of darkness who dragged us all down with him in the apostasy from God, and who can only be resisted in the power of Christ... As Christians we shall hate that spirit because of the love of God's creation in Christ Jesus.

Let us pray that the Spirit of Christ will make all of us those MEN of God, thoroughly furnished unto every good work, also in the political arena of our time. To the man who de-lighteth in the Law of the Lord it is said:

And whatsoever he doeth shall prosper.

About the Contributor

John Hultink, based in Niagara, Ontario, Canada, is the founder of Book Depot in Thorold; the founder of Paideia Press in St. Catharines; and the founder of the reformed magazine *Christian Renewal.* He is also a real estate developer and investor. John has three daughters, all whom are married, and several grandchildren.

ABOUT THE CÁNTARO INSTITUTE
Inheriting, Informing, Inspiring

The Cántaro Institute is a reformed evangelical organization committed to the advancement of the Christian worldview for the reformation and renewal of the church and culture.

We believe that as the Christian church returns to the fount of Scripture as her ultimate authority for all knowing and living, and wisely applies God's truth to every aspect of life, her missiological activity will result in not only the renewal of the human person but also the reformation of culture, an inevitable result when the true scope and nature of the gospel is made known and applied.